This book belongs to

_____

Blessed is the [woman] whose
delight is in the law of the Lord.

Psalm 1:2

A Young Woman's Guide to Discovering Her Bible

ELIZABETH GEORGE

HARVEST HOUSE PUBLISHERS
EUGENE, OREGON

Cover by Dugan Design Group, Bloomington, Minnesota

Cover photos © crazypixels20 / Fotolia; Dugan Design Group

Cover illustration © eugenia / Fotolia

A YOUNG WOMAN'S GUIDE TO DISCOVERING HER BIBLE
Copyright © 2014 Elizabeth George
Published by Harvest House Publishers
Eugene, Oregon 97402
www.harvesthousepublishers.com

Library of Congress Cataloging-in-Publication Data
George, Elizabeth, 1944-
A young woman's guide to discovering her Bible / Elizabeth George.
    pages cm
Includes bibliographical references.
ISBN 978-0-7369-1781-0 (pbk.)
ISBN 978-0-7369-4273-7 (eBook)
1. Bible--Textbooks. 2. Christian teenagers—Religious life--Textbooks. 3 Teenage girls—Religious life—Textbooks. I. Title.
BS605.3.G46 2014
220.6'1—dc23

2014015595

Printed in the United States of America

19 20 21 22 / VP-JH / 10 9 8 7 6 5 4 3

For my precious granddaughters,
   Taylor Zaengle
   Katie Seitz
   Grace Seitz
   Lily Seitz

May you...
   Study the Bible to be wise;
   Believe it to be safe;
   Practice it to be holy.
   Study it through,
      pray it in,
      work it out,
      note it down,
      pass it on.[1]

Contents

1

Discovering Treasure

I will never, ever forget purchasing my first Bible. I was 28 years old and it was my first Sunday in church as a brand-new Christian. There I sat, in a Bible-teaching church...without a Bible! Every time the pastor said, "Turn in your Bible to..." and gave a Scripture reference, the entire auditorium sounded as if each person were unwrapping a gift—you could hear the sound of paper crinkling as everyone sifted through the pages in their Bibles to locate the designated verse.

And then, after a brief pause to give us time to find the verse, a miracle occurred—the pastor taught us what the verse meant.

Never before had I experienced this! At age 12 I had received a Bible when I officially joined my family's local church. But I have to confess, I never read that Bible. I had no idea what it was or where to start reading. I never used it, because...what in the world was I supposed to do with it?

No wonder that beautiful engraved-with-my-name-on-it Bible ended up on a bookshelf gathering dust—for 16 years!

Discovering Treasure

But on that glorious day as a new believer in Christ, I purchased a Bible. I was clueless about the many different versions, translations, and paraphrases of the Bible. I also knew nothing about red-letter versions, hardcover or paperback, bonded or genuine leather bindings. And I had never heard about chronological Bibles or Bibles with indented book tabs or study notes. Eek! It was overload!

So what did I do?

I asked the man at the checkout counter in the church's bookstore to "Just give me a Bible like that man is preaching out of."

He grinned, and I could tell he knew exactly what Bible to get for me. While he was pulling one off the shelf, I noticed a glass bowl next to the cash register. I couldn't miss it because it was filled with brilliant colored highlighter pens.

I just stood there, looking at the many wonderful colors, and prayed, "God, I'm the new kid on the block, and I don't know anything about You. I'm going to purchase a gold highlighter pen and start tomorrow marking everything in my new Bible that teaches me something about You."

With a gold highlighter pen in hand, I looked again at the plethora of colors and prayed, "And God, I don't know anything about being a Christian woman, Christian wife, or Christian mom. I'm also going to purchase a pink highlighter pen and start tomorrow marking everything in my new Bible that has to do with women and instructions to me as a woman."

Well, praise God, He answered my prayers! The very next day, when I cracked open my new Bible and started reading chapter 1 in the book of Genesis, I struck gold. Here's what I found, and I want you to take a look too.

The first verse I marked with my gold highlighter was Genesis 1:1. With your pen or pencil or maybe a highlighter pen, mark what you learn about God in this one verse.

> In the beginning God created the heavens and the earth.

What solid fact about the origin of the world does this verse reveal?

_____

_____

As I continued reading in Genesis 1, the first verse I marked with my pink highlighter was Genesis 1:27. With your pen or pencil or maybe a highlighter pen (maybe pink?), mark what you learn about yourself as a woman.

> God created mankind in his own image, in the image of God he created them; male and female he created them.

What do you learn about God in this verse?

_____

_____

What do you learn about man and woman?

_____

_____

As a young woman, I'm sure you hear a l-o-t about self-image. But let's consider "God-image." How does this verse help you with the way you can and should view yourself? Or, put another way, how would you complete this sentence?

I am created by _____

and in the image of _____

Got Problems?

Believe me, I know from my own growing-up years and from raising two daughters that the teen years are challenging ones. Often it seems like everything in your life is spinning and constantly changing, and it's hard to get your feet and emotions grounded—and then the next big change comes along! At other times it seems like the whole world has stopped turning on its axis. Every day is the same old, same old. Nothing ever changes, and it doesn't look like it ever will. Day after day is the same repeated day. Time is standing still.

I've heard the heart-cries of thousands of teen girls, and here are just a few of their questions and issues:

"What am I going to do about this problem?"

"My problem hurts so much I'm not sure I can make it through another day."

"Why is it so hard to find a friend? Is something wrong with me?"

"I hate my life. It's the same thing day after day—family, chores, school, homework."

"I feel so stifled. I can't go anywhere or do anything without my parents' permission and
involvement."

These are very personal and painful problems and yet, at the
same time, they are "common" problems (says 1 Corinthians
10:13). Thank goodness, because that means there's hope!

No matter what your life situation is, God has help and
answers. No matter how bad things seem or become, when
you are faithful to dig into the treasure of God's Word each
day and look for His help with your problems, as well as His
instructions on how to live the way He wants you to live, you
will enjoy life more. Day by day, God comes to your aid with
encouragement, comfort, guidelines, and wisdom for han-
dling your difficult and stressful situations.

And best of all, you have *Him*—all of Him one-on-one—
when you read His Word! Here are some verses I came across
and marked with my gold highlighter as I continued reading
forward in my Bible. What do you learn about God in these
verses?

Have I not commanded you? Be strong and courageous. Do not be afraid; do not be discouraged, for the Lord your God will be with you
wherever you go (Joshua 1:9).

God... _____

_____

_____

Now read the verse again. Because of what this scripture tells you about God, how can—and should—you approach your challenges and your problems?

_____

_____

_____

Read the verse one more time. We'll talk about "commands" later, but for now, write out God's positive commands:

"Be… _____

_____ "

Also write out God's negative commands:

"Do not… _____

_____ "

What do you learn about God in this next verse?

> Even though I walk through the darkest valley,
> I will fear no evil, for you are with me; your rod
> and your staff, they comfort me (Psalm 23:4).

God… _____

_____

_____

Read the verse again. Because of what this scripture tells you about God, what effect should it have on you?

_____

_____

_____

What do you learn about God from Psalm 147:3, and how does this comfort you?

> He heals the brokenhearted and binds up their wounds.

God... _____

_____

_____

And what do you learn from Isaiah 41:10?

> Do not fear, for I am with you; do not be dismayed, for I am your God. I will strengthen you and help you; I will uphold you with my righteous right hand (Isaiah 41:10).

God... _____

_____

_____

Once again, read through Isaiah 41:10. What are God's commands?

—

—

Next, read Romans 8:38-39.

> I am convinced that neither death nor life, nei-
> ther angels nor demons, neither the present nor
> the future, nor any powers, neither height nor
> depth, nor anything else in all creation, will be
> able to separate us from the love of God that is
> in Christ Jesus our Lord.

How sure and powerful is God's love?

_____

_____

> All Scripture is God-breathed and is useful for
> teaching, rebuking, correcting and training in
> righteousness, so that the servant of God may
> be thoroughly equipped for every good work
> (2 Timothy 3:16-17).

What is the source of all Scripture, and how does it help you?

_____

_____

_____

What is the end goal of God's Word in your life?

_____

_____

A Few Facts About the Bible

I hope you are beginning to sense how excited I was when God's Word began to come alive and minister to me and give me direction. And more than that, I hope you are getting excited too. The few verses we have looked at so far in this chapter are packed with truths that can change your life! They can encourage you when your days are tough, when you are sad, when things aren't going so well at home or school or in your friendships.

The Bible isn't just a book to own and set on a shelf to gather dust (like I did with my Bible). No, it's alive and real—and relevant to all of life with answers for all of life's questions! Once the Bible became the main focal point in my life, I began to understand why it is so special.

Untold volumes of books have been written about the unique nature of the Bible. Here are some important facts that you can know right away and count on forever.

Fact #1: The Bible is supernatural. It is the Word of God. What do these verses tell you about the Bible?

> Above all, you must understand that no prophecy of Scripture came about by the prophet's own interpretation of things. For prophecy never had its origin in the human will, but prophets,

though human, spoke from God as they were carried along by the Holy Spirit (2 Peter 1:20-21).

_____

_____

Fact #2: The Bible is forever. You are probably quite familiar with fads. Clothing styles come and go. Music styles change—and so do hairstyles! Popular authors and book titles turn over regularly. It's easy to wonder if anything is permanent—whether you can put your trust in anything or anyone. Well, God Himself teaches us that we can indeed trust fully in Him and His Word. What do these scriptures tell you about the Bible? What can you count on as promised in these verses?

> The plans of the LORD stand firm forever, the purposes of his heart through all generations (Psalm 33:11).

_____

_____

> The grass withers and the flowers fall, but the word of our God endures forever (Isaiah 40:8).

_____

_____

Fact #3: The Bible is useful. The Bible says God "does not lie" (Titus 1:2). Therefore, since God has communicated to us through His Word, the Bible, we can trust what the Bible says about itself, about God, and how it can change lives. Read Psalm 19:7-11 below and circle each claim the Bible makes for itself. Then underline how useful it can be to you. (A quick note: The psalmist used many different terms to refer to God's Word, the Bible.)

> 7 The law of the LORD is perfect,
>   refreshing the soul.
>   The statutes of the LORD are trustworthy,
>   making wise the simple.
> 8 The precepts of the LORD are right,
>   giving joy to the heart.
>   The commands of the LORD are radiant,
>   giving light to the eyes.
> 9 The fear of the LORD is pure,
>   enduring forever.
>   The decrees of the LORD are firm,
>   and all of them are righteous.
> 10 They are more precious than gold,
>   than much pure gold;
>   they are sweeter than honey,
>   than honey from the honeycomb.
> 11 By them your servant is warned;
>   in keeping them there is great reward.

Yes, There's Help for Your Life

I listed some problems and complaints shared with me by many young adult women, and I'm sure you could add a few of your own. Sometimes it's easy to wonder where, oh where to go for help. But God has answers and advice for your every need, your every difficulty, your every sorrow. He has help for your life. Here's what God says in Psalm 119:9-10:

> How can a young person stay on the path of purity? By living according to your word. I seek you with all my heart; do not let me stray from your commands.

According to these verses, how can you avoid problems, stay out of trouble, and walk on the right path?

_____

_____

_____

What was the heart-cry or prayer of the person who wrote these verses?

_____

_____

_____

Once again, as we begin to move through some traditional methods used to study the Bible, you will learn a lot about commands. Do you want help for your life? The Bible can help you, but only if you obey its commands. For now, just remember: Every time you look at or handle a scripture, ask this question: "Is there a command for me to obey?"

What commands are given in these verses?

> Like newborn babies, crave pure spiritual milk,
> so that by it you may grow up in your salvation
> (1 Peter 2:2).

_____

_____

(A quick note: "spiritual milk" refers to the Word of God.)

And why?

_____

_____

_____

> Grow in the grace and knowledge of our Lord
> and Savior Jesus Christ. To him be glory both
> now and forever! Amen (2 Peter 3:18).

_____

_____

_____

My Prayer for You

It's impossible to count the number of times I've heard Christians say, "I just want to know God," or heard them pray, "Lord, I want to know You." These are the desires of my heart too. But knowing God doesn't come from sitting on a mountaintop somewhere looking off into space. Knowing God comes from reading what God reveals about Himself in His Word, the Bible. Knowing God means wanting and seeking information about Him. That's what helps you grow spiritually. And that, my new friend, is why I'm so excited for you to join with me in this mutual quest to know God. This was the apostle Paul's prayer for all believers—and it is my prayer for you:

> This is my prayer: that your love may abound more and more in knowledge and depth of insight, so that you may be able to discern what is best and may be pure and blameless for the day of Christ (Philippians 1:9-10).

Looking at Your Life

Have you ever taken a class on proper etiquette? Growing up in a Southern state meant that I was expected to take some of these classes. My teachers would show and tell our little group of awkward new teens exactly how we were to act and speak and dress and behave. These instructors told us every week, "You can always have confidence when you know the right thing to do and the right way to act."

Needless to say, those classes helped me tremendously as a young woman-in-the-making to have more confidence in social settings and in interpersonal communication and interaction. They are still helping me to this day.

But nothing compares to the remarkable day when I picked up my Bible for the first time and began to read God's living Word and started highlighting verses about God and my role as a woman. That red-letter day, God's Word became my spiritual teacher in knowing the right things to do and the right way to act as a believer in Jesus Christ. Only God, His Son, and the Holy Spirit can teach you and me about "godly" conduct and about "godliness" and "Christlikeness."

As we work our way through this book on how to understand "The Book" and discover the delightful, astounding treasures that can be found there, I hope and pray you will gain the same kind of spiritual confidence for living your life that I have experienced. It has been a great adventure for me, and I know it will be just as great an adventure for you as you develop a better understanding of how to study and put its truths to work in your heart and life.

2

First Things First

I'm sitting at my desk—writing, of course—and thinking of you! I'm wishing I knew how your spiritual journey has unfolded. How you found out about Jesus and His offer of forgiveness and salvation and an incredible new life. Also, what kind of church do you attend? Are your parents Christians or not? Was this book a gift or part of a study your youth group is going through? How has God orchestrated your spiritual growth?

I know your story isn't like mine. As the saying goes, "There are many roads to Jesus, but only one way to God." And that is through His Son, Jesus Christ. In Scripture, Jesus tells us, "No one comes to the Father except through me" (John 14:6). Whatever your path has been, and whatever means God used to call you to Himself, I hope you thank and praise Him in your heart with every living breath you take!

For me, as I said earlier, God opened the door to my heart at age 28. Once my husband and I found a strong, dynamic church, we purchased our first Bibles as a couple. By this time, we had already been married eight years. After floundering and failing—and flailing!—as spouses and the parents of two little ones, we dove into those brand-new Bibles. We just couldn't get enough! For the first time we had guidelines for life, for marriage, and for parenting. We knew we needed help, and we drank deeply and often from the living water of the Word. We were such babes! I mean, we didn't know *any*thing about the Bible, not even the ages-old stories of Jesus and the great Bible heroes. That is why writing a book about understanding your Bible is so important to me.

We were so needy and for that reason absolutely loved God's Word and set a goal to read through our shiny new Bibles in a year. After doing that for several years, we began to realize that there were additional steps we could take as we read through the Bible that would give us an even greater understanding of God's message for us.

I have to say, I can't think of anything that I resisted as I read and studied. I had a need to know. I had to get my life on track as well as work on my marriage and family—right away! I had issues and behaviors that needed radical help.

Reality Check

Okay—so I'm sure you get the message: You need to read and study your Bible too, right? But wait...you are thinking about all the urgent, important, necessary, and even a few fun things that you're facing this bright new day, and you're realizing that unless you start cutting out a few things, you won't get it all done, especially if you take some time to read your Bible. So guess what? The budding time manager in you starts lopping things off, usually starting with your Bible. You say to yourself, *I'm sure I'll have some time at lunch, or during a*

*break, maybe during study hall, or I'm sure there will be some
time this evening to read my Bible.*

And guess what usually happens? Even though you mean
well, by the end of the day, you've been so busy that you still
haven't taken the time to read from God's Word.

So what can you do? First, it helps to know why it's so
important for you to read your Bible. When you realize how
necessary it is, then you'll set aside time to make it happen. A
good starting point is 2 Timothy 3:16, which says, "All Scripture
is given by inspiration of God, and is profitable" (NKJV). Or as
the NIV Bible says, "All Scripture is God-breathed and is useful."

Look up *profitable* in your dictionary and write its meaning below:

_____

_____

_____

Now, what can you say about all that other "stuff" you did
all day—can you say any of it was truly profitable? I'm sure
some of it was, but I'm also guessing some of it wasn't. However, you can be assured that *every* time you read God's Word,
you are involved in a profitable activity. This is actually a no-
brainer: You can make sure every day gets off to a profitable
start by spending time with God.

Buying Back Time

As you read along, you may be thinking, *I can see the
importance of reading and studying God's Word, but I am so*

incredibly busy! I've got homework, music lessons, soccer prac-
tice, and I'm on the debate team. My list of activities is endless.
There's just no way to fit in time to study my Bible!

Well, my friend, you have just defined the problem, and
a problem defined is a problem half-solved. The only way to
make time for God's Word is to "buy back time." How can this
be done? If the Bible is as important to you as you claim, then
you must choose to get out of bed about 15 minutes earlier
than normal. This is how you buy back time! By getting out of
bed earlier, you'll have time to spend with God, and you can
draw on God for all the things (like positive attitudes, motivation, commitment, and energy) you are going to need today.

For instance, you can ask God for strength. Whoever has
enough of it? And wisdom—your every decision and encounter requires wisdom. Joy—sure, you can plaster on a phony
smile, and it's hard to have joy when your days are too full,
but God is the giver of joy, His joy. And discipline—we can
make all the to-do lists in the world and painstakingly create
a schedule in fine, minute-by-minute detail, but it is God who
spurs us on to follow through and to keep on keeping on.

Your choice to take time in God's Word on the front end
of your fresh new day is vital. Even with all your planning and
preparation, your day is still an unknown. But one thing you
know for sure about the day ahead is that it will—it will!—
include roadblocks, trials, challenges, surprises, heartaches,
and lots of decisions to make.

So before your day gets going or gets out of hand, and
before the day's demands assault you, and before people
invade your solitude and space, seek the Lord. Spend time with

Him. This one step will really set the tone of your day…and your voice…and your words…and your actions…and your attitudes…and the way you treat people—starting right at home with your own family!

Once you're up, you will want to make God your Number One priority. You will want to choose to put first things first. You will want to meet with Him before the day gets rolling.

As I said, sometimes we think we just don't have time to stop and spend some of it with God. I mean, we have people to see, places to go, and things to do! But oh how wrong we are. The Bible is a special book. In fact, it's the greatest book ever written! And if you are a Christian, God's Spirit—the Holy Spirit—speaks to you as you read God's Word. That's why it's so important for you to spend time reading God's Word.

When you read the Bible you will think differently. You will live differently. You will grow spiritually. And you will be blessed—truly, deeply blessed. Don't you think these benefits and blessings are worth the simple effort of getting up a few minutes early and getting into God's Word? And here's another compelling reason: Jesus said that "apart from me you can do nothing" (John 15:5).

Please don't choose to be a "nothing" woman. Get up and read your Bible so God shines through you. Then go out and bear fruit for Jesus!

Count Your Blessings

The blessings abound when you take time to turn to God's Word. Read the following verses and describe how God's Word can help you:

> I have hidden your word in my heart that I might not sin against you (Psalm 119:11).

_____

_____

Scripture teaches and instructs you. It rebukes you and points out sin in your life. It corrects you and straightens out your thinking and choices. And it trains and equips you to live for God, helping you choose to do what is right (see 2 Timothy 3:16 below).

> Your word is a lamp for my feet, a light on my path (Psalm 119:105).

_____

_____

My husband and I take our morning walks early while it is dark. So we take a flashlight for safety and guidance. But back when Psalm 119 was written, the light people used was provided by a wick that was soaked in oil and placed into a crude piece of pottery that was held in a person's palm. Whether the light you use comes from a wick, a flashlight, or the face of your cell phone, it gives you confidence as you move forward in a dark setting. It also keeps you from wandering off the path. And it prevents you from tripping over an obstacle and suffering an injury.

When it comes to your walk with God and making right choices so you are following Him with all your heart, God's

Word points the way. It gives you the truth you need for making right decisions and good moral choices.

> All Scripture is God-breathed and is useful for teaching, rebuking, correcting and training in righteousness (2 Timothy 3:16).

List the six things God's Word claims for itself in 2 Timothy 3:16.

—

—

—

—

—

—

There are very few things you can be completely sure of. But the Bible is in its own rare, for-sure category. "All" of the Bible—100 percent of it—is 100 percent from God, 100 percent inspired by Him, 100 percent true, 100 percent pure, and 100 percent helpful and useful. You never have to doubt anything you read in the Bible, and you never have to doubt its ability to better your life.

What does the Bible prepare you to do for others, according to 2 Timothy 3:17?

...so that the servant of God may be thoroughly
equipped for every good work.

_____

_____

What a great list of incredible results the Word of God can
have in our lives! My favorite words in this verse are "thoroughly," and "every." Think about it: God's Word makes you
"capable and proficient in everything [you] are called to be
or do."[1] It "thoroughly" equips and enables you to live righteously. And this equipping extends to your service in "every"
good work. Wow, that "thoroughly" covers "every" need!

What else can you expect from the Bible?

> The word of God is alive and active...it judges
> the thoughts and attitudes of the heart (Hebrews
> 4:12).

_____

_____

_____

The Bible sharpens your discernment or judgment. As you
read the Bible, dramatic things happen. Just as you cannot be
near a fire without feeling its warmth, you cannot read the
Bible and not be affected by it. It is alive! And it is powerful! It
is dynamite. Whenever you approach the Word of God, the
ground is already rumbling.

So go ahead and prepare for your world to be rocked!
God's Word will—it will!—change your life. And one of those

changes will have to do with your perspective on life issues. You will view the world and your decisions the way God views them. You will catch yourself thinking about things the way God thinks about them. You will be more sensitive to the way you are choosing to live and the choices you are making as Scripture sifts through and reveals your thoughts and the motives of your heart.

Finally, and most important of all, as in the life of young Timothy, how can the Bible direct you for all eternity?

> From infancy you [Timothy] have known the Holy Scriptures, which are able to make you wise for salvation through faith in Jesus Christ (2 Timothy 3:15).

_____

_____

_____

The Bible gives instructions for eternal life. No other book can offer this kind of assistance. It would be foolish for any person caught in a collapsing building to disregard the exit signs that would lead them toward safety. That's exactly what the Bible offers to a smart young woman like you—perfect, sound guidance.

Getting into God's Word

Can you grasp why making the choice to spend time with God in His Word is so important? Getting into the Bible and having a quiet time alone with God causes you to grow—to grow in the knowledge of Him, which then helps you grow in making better choices and becoming more like Jesus. How does this happen? It's an inside job! The Bible actually changes your heart.

So what can you do to make sure you don't miss out on the miracle of a spiritual makeover every single day? Here are a few steps you can take to help you keep going and keep growing in your love for God's Word and your understanding of the Bible. Every time you take these steps, you are making the choice to make time with God a priority—your Number One priority!

Read it. I could add, just read it. Start anywhere. The only wrong way to read the Bible is not to read it. You can find Bible reading schedules in many Bibles. In fact, there's one in the back of this book on pages 207-14.

Study it. This is yet another way to dig deeper into your Bible. And this is the objective of this book—to help you get to know God better as you study His Word.

Desire it. You already know firsthand the importance of physical food. Well, you need to view the spiritual food of the Bible as having that same importance…only greater! As Job declared, "I have treasured the words of his mouth [God's teaching] more than my daily bread" (Job 23:12).

Storing Up Treasure

How can you store up the treasure you discover in your Bible?

Memorize it. Most young people have no problem at all

memorizing the lyrics to a favorite song or hymn. When I go to my local gym, I see young women listening to music through their earbuds and mouthing the words to the songs they're hearing. Some of them sing out loud. The words are there in their heads, working through their minds, and coming out of their mouths. Well, that's how easy and natural memorizing God's Word can be…if you choose to make it a part of your life.

There is no better way to live God's way than to have His Word in your heart and in your mind…and then carry it out in your actions. If God's Word is within you, He will use it to help you with your struggles, relationships, and choices.

So why memorize Bible verses? To begin, what did God tell Joshua to do when he became Moses' successor?

> Meditate on it [the Book of the Law] day and night, so that you may be careful to do everything written in it. Then you will be prosperous and successful (Joshua 1:8).

_____

_____

_____

(A quick note: To "meditate" on His Word "day and night" means God expected Joshua to know His Word by heart.)

How would this help Joshua in his new position? For one thing, it would supply Joshua, the warrior and leader of God's army, the courage he needed to lead God's people into battle and into their new homeland—a land filled with hostile occupants who in no way wanted to give up their homes and property.

Knowing God's law would also help Joshua make right choices and judge righteously among the people.

And here's a big boon: Joshua had a serious problem with fear. (Can you relate?) God's Word was loaded with powerful promises that would help Joshua overcome his fears and serve God and His people more effectively.

We looked at Psalm 119:11 earlier, but this is a good time to review it. How does the Bible help you when you memorize Scripture?

> I have hidden your word in my heart that I might not sin against you.

_____

_____

_____

Bonus question: How does James 4:17 define sin?

_____

_____

_____

The advice to hide God's Word in your heart so that you might avoid sin is good advice for men and women of all ages! It is also a forever truth. This was the observation of the great preacher D.L. Moody as he put this notation beside Psalm 119:11 in his Bible:

> Either this book will keep you from sin, or sin
> will keep you from this book.[2]

Psalm 119:11 makes it clear that when you put God's Word in your heart, it becomes a safeguard against sin. It will protect you from making wrong choices and suffering the painful consequences that go along with making wrong choices.

As I studied the language in Psalm 119:11, I discovered that "to hide" means to store, to treasure. Sometimes we act as if God's Word were some ill-tasting medicine that is hard to swallow. But Psalm 19:10 describes God's Word as "sweeter than honey, than honey from the honeycomb." When you take time to memorize it, it'll be available to you when you need to pull it out.

I'm always humbled by the young teenager, Mary, who became the mother of our Savior, Jesus. She was passionate about memorizing portions of the Bible, and was faithful to do it! How do we know this? Because when Mary opened her mouth to praise God for the blessing of the Savior, out poured Bible verses—at least 15 references to scriptures from the Old Testament (Luke 1:46-55). These were verses and truths Mary, as a girl, had memorized on purpose (memorizing Scripture is always a choice) and learned by heart. Because they were within her, they became her prayer and praise language. Truly, when she opened her mouth, her lips leaked God's Word. And it was His Word in her heart that helped her live out God's plan for her to become Jesus' mother.

Joshua and Mary's examples urge us across the centuries to get started on this spiritual discipline of hiding God's Word in our hearts. So what can you do today to make this happen?

First, ask yourself: "What are some of my favorite verses

in the Bible?" Pick several. Write one out. Then memorize it. Make it your own! I keep a stack of 3" x 5" cards in my kitchen drawer. Then I can grab one anytime to write out a fresh, new, exciting verse to memorize. These cards then go with me everywhere for learning or reviewing all day long, anywhere, anytime.

Or you can put your verses on your cell phone. I know you're never without your phone! During your down minutes, instead of checking Facebook or email first, refresh yourself by reviewing the verse you are memorizing. If you can't think of a verse, use one of the two below to get launched. I picked the first one because it is so helpful to me and to most of the women I know as we face our daily challenges. And I chose the second one to remind us to consult God before we make our choices—so that He can guide us to the right choices, His choices!

> Be strong and courageous. Do not be afraid; do not be discouraged, for the LORD your God will be with you wherever you go (Joshua 1:9).

> In all your ways submit to him, and he will make your paths straight (Proverbs 3:6).

Looking at Your Life

Just think—the Bible is all yours all the time. It's the ultimate source of truth and advice and power. And it's the ultimate beauty treatment starting from the inside out! As God's Word makes its way into your heart, it energizes you. And it changes your views about yourself, about people, and about the things that are happening in your life.

Your better life is as close and as easy as making the choice to pick up your Bible each day, open it up, and take a few minutes to let God speak directly to you. When you do this, you'll know what to do and how to handle everything that comes along. You'll receive your marching orders from God's love letter to you.

The Best Kind of Studying

If you're a Christian, it makes sense that you'd want to learn as much as you could about Jesus Christ and His Word…Think about it—of all the things you learn in your life, what's the most important? It's not algebra or biology! Although studying these subjects is important and necessary, the most important thing is to know who God is and what He wants you to do in your life. And the more you learn about Him, the more you feel secure and have strength for whatever challenges you have to face. Reading the Bible is the best kind of studying![3]

3

Stories for Your Heart

Every girl loves a good story, especially if it tugs on her heart and has a happy ending. If you are looking for good stories that send life messages to your heart, the Bible is the ultimate place to look! More than half of the Bible is what's called narrative literature. This type of literature consists of historical events rehearsed, recorded, and passed down from generation to generation. What happened to God's people is written down in the Bible so we can read these stories about God's power and compassion. Through the narratives in the Bible we can know the truth so we don't forget God's work in choosing and protecting a people—the Jewish people—from whom ultimately the Messiah, Jesus Christ, would be born.

As we step into this chapter, I want you to take a peek at a few of the incredible narrative stories about real women in the Bible—especially young women like you, women in their teens. They each faced a dire crisis, and they each were brave and courageous as they trusted God and did the right thing. But before we get to those stories, let's talk about the variety of literature in the Bible and questions you can ask when you read and study the Bible.

~ BIBLE STUDY 101 ~
VARIETY OF LITERATURE IN THE BIBLE

If you were to ask people what two classes they detested the most in school, many would quickly say English literature and English grammar and composition. Maybe that's why so many people can't, won't, or don't want to read the Bible. Maybe it's because taking the time to read and understand the Bible reminds them too much of their literature and grammar courses. (Actually, these were some of my favorite classes. I even got to teach them to grades 7-12!)

To discover what's so wonderful about the Bible, you must approach it like any other book. Most books contain only one type of literature, like fiction, or nonfiction, or poetry. One of the reasons some people have a hard time understanding the Bible is because it is made up of several different types of literature. It contains poetry, prophecy, teaching, and narrative—or, as your English teacher would call it, prose.

~ BIBLE STUDY 101 ~
NARRATIVE LITERATURE

Much of the Bible, including the Old Testament, the Gospels (Matthew, Mark, Luke, and John), and Acts is a type of literature called narrative. Narratives are stories, and in the case of the Bible, God's story—a story that is utterly true and crucially important. Bible narratives tell you about things that happened—but not just any ordinary things. They are special because their purpose is to show God at work in His creation and among His people. This narrative literature showcases God and helps you to understand and appreciate Him. This literature gives you a picture of God's care and protection and provides illustrations of many other lessons that are important to your life.

~ BIBLE STUDY 101 ~
OBSERVATION

Once you read a verse or a portion of the Bible, the first step in discovering the truths and teachings within them is called the process of OBSERVATION.

Observation demands that you learn to ask the right questions of the scriptures you are studying. If you ever take a journalism class at school or college, your teachers will probably send you out to report on an event either at the school or in the local area. Your report would have to include answers to the following kinds of questions—often referred to as the "WH" questions. These questions are tools that will help you get the most out of what you read in the Bible. They will aid you in the Bible study step of observation.

Who?

What?

Where?

When?

Later we will get to

Why? (interpretation) and

So What? (application)

Getting the Most Out of a Pink Passage

Armed with my new Bible, my goal as a baby Christian was to read one chapter a day. Well, on Day 3, I was blown away by the opening of Genesis chapter 3. This is a very significant passage for all Christians, and for all women. This foundational passage is about the first woman ever alive. As soon as I started into the first verse of Genesis 3 and spotted the word "woman," out came my pink marker.

Here now is the passage—Genesis 3:1-7—with a few questions for you. As you read it and work your way through it, keep in mind that this is an example of a narrative passage.

> 1 Now the serpent was more crafty than any of the wild animals the LORD God had made. He said to the woman, "Did God really say, 'You must not eat from any tree in the garden'?"
>
> 2 The woman said to the serpent, "We may eat fruit from the trees in the garden,
>
> 3 but God did say, 'You must not eat fruit from the tree that is in the middle of the garden, and you must not touch it, or you will die.'"
>
> 4 "You will not certainly die," the serpent said to the woman.
>
> 5 "For God knows that when you eat from it your eyes will be opened, and you will be like God, knowing good and evil."

6 When the woman saw that the fruit of the tree was good for food and pleasing to the eye, and also desirable for gaining wisdom, she took some and ate it. She also gave some to her husband, who was with her, and he ate it.

7 Then the eyes of both of them were opened, and they realized they were naked; so they sewed fig leaves together and made coverings for themselves.

Who are the three characters in this story, how are they described, and what is each one doing?

—

—

—

What is happening? Or, what's going on or taking place?

_____

_____

Where is this happening? (There may or may not be references to place or location.)

_____

_____

When is this happening? (There may or may not be references to time.)

_____

_____

How did the man and the woman try to cover their sin of disobedience to God?

_____

_____

Based on these verses, how would you answer this question: How did sin enter God's perfect world?

_____

_____

_____

In the pages ahead you will learn more about examining surrounding scriptures (called *context*), but for now look at Genesis 2:16-17.

Exactly what did God say about what the man and woman *could* eat?

_____

_____

Exactly what did God say about what *could not* be eaten?

_____

_____

_____

What did God say would happen if His instructions were not followed?

_____

_____

Who did God give this information to?

_____

Personal application: List the lessons you can learn from Genesis 3:1-7:

As a woman:

_____

_____

_____

About the serpent and his tactics:

_____

_____

_____

About temptation:

_____

_____

_____

About sin and disobedience:

_____

_____

_____

Some Things to Think About

How could Eve have responded differently and resisted the temptation to eat the forbidden fruit?

> By following the same guidelines we can follow. First, we must realize that being tempted, in and of itself, is not a sin. We have not sinned until we give in to the temptation. Then, to resist temptation, we must (1) pray for strength to resist, (2) run (sometimes literally), and (3) say no when confronted with what we know is wrong.[1]

The serpent (Satan) tempted Eve by getting her to doubt God's greatness. He suggested that God was strict, stingy, and selfish for not wanting Eve to share his knowledge of good and evil. Satan made Eve forget all that God had given her. Instead, he got her to focus on the one thing she couldn't have. We fall into trouble too when we focus on the few things we don't have rather than on the countless things God has given us. The next time you are feeling sorry for yourself over what you don't have, consider all you do have and thank God.[2]

What You Are at Home Is What You Are

Do you have brothers and sisters? And do they get on your nerves? Is your little sister always getting into your things—your makeup, your jewelry, your hair stuff, even your diary or personal journal? Or do you have a little brother you are tempted to address as "Brat"? He can't sit still. He breaks just about everything he touches. He's always running and roughhousing. And he's soooo loud!

How you perceive and respond to your siblings reveals your heart and who you really are. How you treat your brothers and sisters is a sure giveaway of your true character. As the saying goes, what you are at home is what you are! It's easy to be all peaches and cream when you are with your friends at school or church. Everybody gets a huge smile, a compliment, a friendly question about how things are going, and maybe even a hug. Why, you are the sweetest girl anyone has ever met. Wow!

And meanwhile, at home, you can get mean and ugly toward your brothers and sisters. You resent them because Mom and Dad have assigned you to help them in a variety of ways. You sneer at them, put them down, rag on them, maybe even physically push them around. In your opinion—which is freely expressed—they can't do anything right. It doesn't take any words for you to communicate that your life would be a whole lot better if they had never been born.

Let's face it. You either love and enjoy that pesky little sister and overzealous brother, or you despise them, ignore them, and have as little to do with them as possible.

Well, meet Miriam. She's a young woman I met in the Bible as soon as I got to the book of Exodus in my daily Bible reading. She was about 12 years old when she first appears in Exodus 2. Miriam was the older sister to two brothers—Aaron and Moses. Here's her backstory:

There was a time in Israel's history when Pharaoh, the ruler of Egypt, decreed that every male baby born was to be killed. Enter baby Moses, who was born to Jochebed and Amram while Pharaoh ruled. When Jochebed saw how beautiful her baby boy was, she knew she couldn't allow him to die. So she made a tough decision and went into action.

As you read Exodus 2:1-10, grab your favorite pen, pencil, or highlighter pen. Use it to answer the questions that follow the scriptures as you observe the ten verses that make up this passage about the young woman Miriam.

Using the WH questions, read Exodus 2:1-10 and follow the OBSERVATION exercises to discover what kind of girl Miriam was—at home. Here we go!

1 Now a man of the tribe of Levi married a Levite woman,

2 and she became pregnant and gave birth to a son. When she saw that he was a fine child, she hid him for three months.

3 But when she could hide him no longer, she got a papyrus basket for him and coated it with tar and pitch. Then she placed the child in it and put it among the reeds along the bank of the Nile.

4 His sister stood at a distance to see what would happen to him.

5 Then Pharaoh's daughter went down to the Nile to bathe, and her attendants were walking along the riverbank. She saw the basket among the reeds and sent her female slave to get it.

6 She opened it and saw the baby. He was crying, and she felt sorry for him. "This is one of the Hebrew babies," she said.

7 Then his sister asked Pharaoh's daughter, "Shall I go and get one of the Hebrew women to nurse the baby for you?"

8 "Yes, go," she answered. So the girl went and got the baby's mother.

9 Pharaoh's daughter said to her, "Take this baby and nurse him for me, and I will pay you." So the woman took the baby and nursed him.

10 When the child grew older, she took him to Pharaoh's daughter and he became her son. She named him Moses, saying, "I drew him out of the water."

Who are the people?

— Circle the names of every person mentioned in these verses.

What did they do?

— Underline what they did.

Where did this take place?

— Place brackets [ ] around each place mentioned.

When did this take place (both in history and time of day)?

— Bracket [ ] all references to time.

Why did these people do what they did?

— This may or may not be directly stated. Underline any words that tell you why. And feel free to write in the margins of your book.

Character counts! What character qualities do you see in Miriam, a girl who was probably about 12 years old? Sift through each verse, looking specifically for Miriam's qualities, and make a list of them here.

Verse 4—

Verse 7—

Verse 8—

What character qualities do you see in Jochebed, Miriam's mother?

Verse 2—

Verse 3—

Verse 9—

Verse 10—

What character qualities do you see in Pharaoh's daughter?

Verse 6—

Verse 8—

Verse 9—

Verse 10—

Every time you read or study the Bible, or hear it taught in church or in your youth group, remember this: The purpose of Bible study is to change your life. So once you have observed the facts, whatever you do, don't stop there! Go the next step and, based on your observations of what the Bible says, make applications to your own life.

James 1:22 instructs us: "Do not merely listen to the word, and so deceive yourselves. Do what it says."

Then James 1:23-24 adds an illustration to help us understand the importance of applying God's teachings so we grow, change, and are transformed into Christlikeness:

23 Anyone who listens to the word but does not do what it says is like someone who looks at his face in a mirror

24 and, after looking at himself, goes away and immediately forgets what he looks like.

It's great and it's important to study God's Word. But even more important to God is that you do what He says you should do—that you obey Him. You must make it personal.

Making It Personal

Once you have read God's Word and observed it to discover the who, what, where, when, and whys from the Scripture passages, you are ready to make it personal. This step in studying the Bible is APPLICATION. Take time to answer the questions that follow. They are designed to help you to apply God's Word to your life today, to make it personal.

Miriam

What lessons have you learned from Miriam that you want to take away from these ten verses?

_____

_____

_____

How does Miriam's love for her brother convict or encourage you about your attitude toward your siblings?

_____

_____

_____

What will you do today to be more caring and helpful to your brothers and sisters—and to your mom?

_____

_____

_____

Don't you just love Miriam's story—and her heart? She was diligent. She cared about her brother and stayed behind to see what would happen to him. She wasn't thinking about going home and eating a cookie, or resting after her ordeal, or hoping everything would go well for the little guy. No, she stayed to the end. She did everything she could do to make sure he would be okay!

And Miriam was a quick thinker. She came up with a plan when Pharaoh's daughter found her baby brother. She also took the initiative to approach the princess and offer a solution for nourishing the baby. Who better to nurse the baby than his own mother?!

However old you are, you can be a woman of character. You can care about people, beginning right at home with your family. You can go into action when your help is needed. You can be your mom's right-hand person and trusted assistant—her best helper. The choice is yours.

ARE YOU A MONSTER OR A MIRIAM?

Miriam could have resented her little brother, but she loved him. She could have been jealous of the time he as a newborn required from his mother, time which had been spent with Miriam before his arrival. She could have resented that he seemed to cry all the time. And she could have sulked because her mom needed her help with the baby and household chores. You cannot choose your circumstances, but you can always choose the attitude you have toward them. You can choose to be angry and disgusted about your home situation, or you can choose to see God in your circumstances and cheerfully, energetically do all you can to help, love, and care for the people at home.

Pharaoh's Daughter

Think about this young princess's reaction to finding a baby while bathing in the Nile River. Think about her response to Miriam's suggestion for the baby's well-being. Think about her willingness to pay for the baby's care. Think about her adopting the baby and taking him into the palace as her son. What lessons have you learned from Pharaoh's daughter that you want to take away from Exodus 2:1-10?

_____

_____

_____

_____

_____

What will you do today to be more caring, helpful, and compassionate to others who are suffering and in need of help, especially to those you live with at home?

_____

_____

_____

_____

_____

Moses' Mother

Jochebed had a serious decision to make, an idea in mind, faith in God (Hebrews 11:23), and the courage to follow through on her idea. How does her courage impress you? What lessons have you learned from Moses' mother that you want to take away from Exodus 2:1-10?

_____

_____

_____

_____

God, the Unseen Person

Although God is not mentioned in Exodus 2:1-10, how do you see Him at work? How did God use all the people in these verses to save the life of Moses, the man He would use in the future to save His people from their bondage and lead them to the Promised Land?

_____

_____

The Bible tells us to "meditate" on the Scriptures (Joshua 1:8). You can and should meditate on the Scriptures and the person of God. Though He is not seen, He is, and He is with you. And He is actively involved in and at work in your life! As the psalmist exulted in Psalm 48:14, "This God is our God for ever and ever."

Looking at Your Life

If you have brothers or sisters, you can't help but see how they act. You also witness how your parents respond to their actions. And when you watch your siblings say or do something wrong and receive some sort of punishment for it, if you are smart, you will think, *Note to self: Do not make that sort of statement to my parents, or break that rule, or do that which displeases Mom and Dad!* As you watch and learn from the stories of what happens to your brothers or sisters, you learn what to do and what not to do.

You too are writing your own story. How will it read? Will it reveal a young girl like Miriam, who was a helpful daughter and sister? Are you going to grow up to be a woman who follows God with all her heart?

One way to ensure that your story fulfills this hope is to take to heart the stories of the women of the Bible and their examples—women like Eve and Miriam and Jochebed. As Romans 15:4 tells us, "everything that was written in the past was written to teach us."

4

True Beauty

Have you ever thought about who might be the most beautiful woman who ever lived? When a woman's beauty is discussed, most people immediately start thinking of physical beauty. You know, the kind of beauty possessed by someone who might participate in a competition like the Miss America or Miss Universe pageants. Others might think of a famous historical figure like Cleopatra—at least that's how the movie created and billed the star.

But all these speculations would be wrong.

The most beautiful woman who ever lived was the first woman who ever lived, Eve. You've already met her in this book. Eve was beautiful because God created her Himself (Genesis 1:27). God fashioned Eve as the perfect woman to be placed in a perfect world next to the perfect man. She was flawless!

Physically Eve was the most beautiful woman of all time, and that physical beauty would have lasted forever. But her beauty was more than skin-deep. She also possessed inner beauty because she was sinless. Her heart and life were perfectly pure. She always looked gorgeous, never blundered socially but always said the right thing and acted the right way—and she was a perfect complement to the perfect man.

Tragically, Eve lost her perfect inner beauty when she fell into sin and chose to do the one thing God told her and Adam not to do. Oh, she still retained her outer physical beauty for a while. But that beauty was only temporary as she declined physically and grew old and died.

What does all this have to do with our journey toward understanding how to study your Bible? I'm glad you asked! In this chapter you will discover several more principles for understanding your Bible as you survey the life of Esther, another young woman after God's own heart—a woman who was the winner of a beauty contest.

You are in for a real treat—Esther was a thrilling young woman! We are going to dig into the book and life of Esther, and as we do so, you will learn about God's character, His plan for Esther's life, and the history of this remarkable young woman's faith and trust in Him. In her you will discover an example of what true beauty is. But more than that, you will witness what an iron-like courage and devotion to living for God looks like in a real-life young adult woman.

Hang on tight as Esther shows you how to follow God, and how to live—or die—for Him, no matter what the circumstances, and no matter what the cost.

~ BIBLE STUDY 101 ~
CONTEXT

In Bible study, *context* means identifying what happened before and after the verse or verses you are examining. Here you ask and answer the question, "What is the context of the verse or passage of Scripture I am studying?"

There are two main kinds of context.

Near context—This has to do with information stated in the verse, or verses immediately before and after the passage you are studying or reading.

Far context—This refers to the verses leading up to your verse or passage and those following after it. The far context could also include the subject matter in the chapters before or after the passage you are focusing on.

Sometimes context is determined by the theme of the chapter or book of the Bible you are studying. For instance, in Exodus 20 we read about God giving Moses the Ten Commandments. Therefore, any verse you study in Exodus 20 would have its meaning derived from the context of the entire chapter.

Identifying context in Bible study will answer most of your WH questions. Some scholars say that 75 to 90 percent of all your questions in Bible study can be answered by simply looking at the context. That is why knowing the context of a verse or passage is so important.

The Road to Becoming Queen

And now, meet Queen Esther. Actually, when you first meet her, she isn't royalty at all. She's a girl, probably in her teens, a young woman just trying to grow up—at a time when the kingdom of Persia was turned upside down!

What happened? Before you look for the answer to this

question, let's briefly review what we learned earlier in chapter 3 about the all-important step of OBSERVATION.

~ BIBLE STUDY 101 ~
REVIEW OF OBSERVATION

When studying narrative literature in the Bible, you will do a lot of observing of facts and details. Observation requires that you ask and answer these questions:

WHO are the people? If a pronoun such as *he* or *she* is used, read backward to find the identity of the person at hand. How is the person described? Is any information given regarding his or her background or lineage?

WHAT did the people do? Or, WHAT's happening? Is someone teaching? If so, what—and what was the effect of the teaching? Is it a miracle? If so, what happened? Is it a battle? An argument or a debate? If so, who's winning? Is it a travelogue? If so, who's going where…and why?

WHERE did this event or scene take place? Is a country, area, or town mentioned? Is it indoors or outdoors? Are any specific places or cities named? A field? A garden? A house?

WHEN did this event take place (both in history and time of day)? Is a season or day of the week mentioned? Is the time of day morning, noon, evening, or night?

WHY did these people do what they did? This may or may not be directly stated. Is someone suffering? Ill? Disabled? Afraid? Are the people obeying God? Disobeying God? Are they in the midst of a battle?

As you go through each verse in the pages that follow, run through the WH questions and make notes in the spaces provided. Also, remember that not every WH question asked will be answered in the verse you are looking at. As always, whatever you do, don't get discouraged. And don't give up. Just enjoy the thrilling story of Esther—and learn what you can from her.

Ready, Set—Action!

If you've ever been in a play, you know the stage becomes the setting for the drama. The same is true for what we want to highlight in the life of Esther. So let's set the stage for the drama that is about to occur, all drawn from CONSULTATION—from consulting reference books that tell us about the historical background of Esther's story. Read along in your Bible to see what we learn.

> Esther 1:1: Describes the vast region of the context of the book of Esther, including 127 provinces ranging from India to Ethiopia.

> Esther 1:2: Narrows down the region of the context to one place—Susa, the site of one of the king's palaces.

> Esther 1:3-12: Details a six-month-long gathering that ended with a seven-day drinking feast.

In your Bible, locate Esther 1.

What do you learn in verse 9 (which is the beginning of a "pink passage," a passage about women and a woman)?

_____

_____

_____

The Request

Scan through verses 10-12. What request was made of the reigning Queen Vashti, and by whom?

_____

How is Queen Vashti described?

_____

The Response

How did Queen Vashti respond to the request?

_____

How did King Xerxes respond to the queen's answer?

_____

Things start to move rapidly now. Note what occurred in these verses that created a chain of events:

The Results

What happened to Queen Vashti in verse 19?

_____

Outline what happened next in:

Esther 2:2 _____

_____

Esther 2:3 _____

_____

Esther 2:4 _____

_____

The Response

What did King Xerxes think of this proposal?

_____

_____

Meet Esther (Esther 2:5-11)

Now that the stage is set (the CONTEXT), enjoy the thrilling story of Esther and learn from her strength and her many character qualities. She was a young woman in a very tough situation. Yet her inner beauty won the hearts of many, and her faith contributed to the salvation of the Jewish people—God's people!

In Esther 2:5-7, what do you learn about...

Esther's heritage?

_____

_____

_____

_____

Esther's family background?

_____

_____

_____

_____

Esther's name?

_____

_____

(A quick note: CONSULTATION with reference books tells us that Hadassah, meaning "myrtle," was Esther's Hebrew name. Her Persian name [Esther] meant "star."[1])

Esther's appearance?

_____

_____

_____

Read Esther 2:8-14. Write or journal what you learn about Esther in each of these verses:

Verse 8: _____

_____

Verse 9: _____

_____

Verse 10: _____

_____

Verse 11: _____

_____

An Audience with a King (Esther 2:12-14)

Continue with your "journal entries" or your notes from these verses:

Verse 12: _____

_____

Verse 13: _____

_____

Verse 14: _____

_____

Verse 15: _____

_____

As you put together a portrait of young Esther, what do you specifically learn about her in:

Verse 9?

Verse 10?

Verse 15?

A New Queen Is Found (Esther 2:15-18)

At the beginning of this chapter I briefly mentioned beauty pageants. This competition in which Esther was placed is the pageant of all pageants!

According to verses 16-18, what was the outcome?

_____

_____

_____

Fast-forward to a dark day—and a turning point—in Esther's life as queen. Here's a quick look at what was happening:

— Mordecai, Esther's godly cousin, foiled an assassination plot against the king and was honored and rewarded, much to the chagrin of Haman, an evil man who hated all Jews, and especially Mordecai, because he would not bow down to Haman.

— The evil Haman duped the king into issuing a decree that designated one specific day when the people of Persia would be allowed "to destroy, kill, and annihilate all the Jews—young and old, women and children...and to plunder their goods" (Esther 3:13).

— Mordecai sent Esther a copy of the decree and advised her, "Do not think that because you are in the king's house you alone of all the Jews will escape. For if you remain silent at this time, relief and deliverance for the Jews will arise from another place, but you and your father's family will perish. And who knows but that you have come to your royal position for such a time as this?" (Esther 4:13-14).

Now read Esther 4:11 in your Bible. Why did Esther think she could not appeal for help from her husband, the king?

_____

_____

_____

Once Esther decided to approach her husband anyway, she went into preparation mode. What was Number One on her list of preparations according to verse 16, and how did she set it in motion?

_____

_____

_____

Knowing she could be put to death for coming before the king, what brave words did Esther utter (verse 16)?

_____

_____

Read Esther 5:4 to find out Esther's Number Two item on her list of preparations:

_____

_____

Queen Esther entertained her husband, the king, and, the evil Haman by giving two banquets. At the end of the second banquet, she revealed to the king what she knew about Haman's plan to kill her, his queen, as well as all the Jews—all her people. What does Esther 7:7-10 say resulted from the risk Esther took to speak up?

_____

_____

_____

_____

_____

Esther Saves the Day—and the Jews!

But Esther wasn't done. Having Haman dead wouldn't save her people. In Esther 8:3-5, we see Esther falling before the king and begging him to revoke the decree that allowed the people of Persia to murder the Jews. However, because Persian law prohibited a king's decree from being rescinded, all King Xerxes could do was give Mordecai permission to dictate and send a second decree.

According to Esther 8:11-12, what decree was given in the letter Mordecai dictated in the name of the king?

_____

_____

For the grand finale, read Esther 9:16. What happened when the people of Persia sought to kill the Jews?

_____

_____

According to verse 17, what occurred on the following day?

_____

To this day, Jewish people around the world celebrate these events that took place in the book of Esther and observe the Feast of Purim annually to remember the salvation of the Jews from their enemies.

Making It Personal

As you consider what you've learned from the book of Esther, there are several strong messages that can be applied to your life:

— *The importance of family.* No one's home life is perfect. Esther's certainly wasn't—she had no parents... but she had her cousin, Mordecai. Who do you have as family? Cherish them and take every opportunity to strengthen your bonds.

— *The importance of taking wise advice.* As a young woman, Esther exhibited a long list of sterling character qualities. One of the marks of her wisdom was her understanding of the importance of asking others for advice. She asked Mordecai for advice and did what he said. She also did exactly what the person in charge of the king's women advised her about what to wear when going before the king. Do you ask for advice from your parents or youth pastor or a woman you respect? And do you follow through on their counsel? Proverbs says "victory is won through many advisers" and "plans are established by seeking advice" (Proverbs 11:14; 20:18). So ask!

— *The importance of preparation.* Esther was also the queen of preparation and grasped its importance. She prepared herself physically to be presented to the king. She prepared herself spiritually with prayer and fasting before she risked approaching the king without being summoned. And she prepared practically before the two banquets held for King Xerxes and Haman. Do you see your daily time with the Lord as preparing yourself to live for God each day? Do you work in advance of your deadlines?

The Final Act

In every stage play, there is a final act and a final scene right before the lights dim and the curtain falls. Please read Esther 9:29-32 to see the parting picture of Esther and her position of influence. There she stands, forever preserved in the Scriptures, side by side with her righteous cousin Mordecai, assisting the king and watching over the welfare of God's people, the Jews. As one commentator summarized, Esther "broke through cultural norms, stepping outside her expected role to risk her life to help God's people. Whatever your place in life, God can use you. Be open, available, and ready, because God may use you to do what others are afraid even to consider."[2]

Coincidence...or Providence?

What others may call coincidence is known to wise believers as Providence. Esther could have rationalized her unique position in the palace as simply "happenstance" or "a roll of the dice." In fact, it seems she was initially tempted to downplay her role altogether: "I'm not the one to help the Jews. I don't have a chance." Her cousin and adviser, Mordecai, replied by reminding her of her particular place in the larger picture of God's plan. She realized that God had given her beauty, her nationality, her relatives, and her influence in that palace as crucial elements to be used in his service...

Nothing about you is a coincidence—in fact, everything about you is vitally useful for accomplishing God's work. Set aside time this week to take stock of the potential assets you have yet to use in service to God.

What others see as coincidence, faith knows as Providence.[3]

Looking at Your Life

I can't think of a better way for you to look at your life than to look at another young woman who was filled with God's beauty and strength. She was faithful to grow each day in the grace and knowledge of God, a God who called her, fortified her, used her, and loved her to the very end—which was the beginning of life in His very presence...forever. I am praying for you now as you meet Natalie Dyck on the next page.

Is Your Greatest Joy to
Bring a Smile to Your Savior's Face?

How I thank God that in the midst of my writing I came to hear of a woman who fleshed out the exquisite qualities found throughout the book of Esther. She was young—barely 22 years old. Yet in her brief life, her character had grown until its godly beauty reached out and touched forever the lives of those within the fragrance of her life. Her name is Natalie Christine Dyck. (I am purposely using the present tense because our knowledge and memories of her live on and will always affect us deeply.)

Just a few weeks after she graduated from The Master's College in Newhall, California, dear Natalie headed for Tanzania, Africa, where she was to spend the summer using her new degree in education to teach African children the English language and to share about God's love for them. And then, in the sovereign purposes and providence of the "true God who is all knowing, omnipresent, powerful, and in every way perfect" (these are words shared from Natalie's personal journal), on her way to minister alongside her missionary aunt and uncle, Natalie, along with 13 other people, died in a bus accident.

Natalie Dyck was truly a woman of deep inner beauty and strength. It was out of that lovely beauty and powerful faith that Natalie journaled these words: "The greatest joy in my life is to serve my Savior. Everything that I do, say, and think each day needs to be a reflection of the God that I serve. A quote that I have applied personally to my life is, 'My greatest joy in life is to bring a smile to my Savior's face.'"

I wanted you to know about this young woman, Natalie Dyck, this present-day Esther, whose character so abounded with the beauty of the Lord. May her life touch yours, dear one, as it has deeply touched mine through the testimony of so many who knew her well. These truths about reputation versus character that follow on the next page were printed on the program for Natalie's memorial service. May they point you to the value of being a woman of beauty and strength like Natalie, and to the priceless worth of hard-won godly character.

The circumstances amid which you live
determine your reputation;
The truth you believe determines your character.

Reputation is what you are supposed to be;
Character is what you are.

Reputation is the photograph;
Character is the face.

Reputation comes over one from without;
Character grows from within.

Reputation is what you have when you come into
a new community;
Character is what you have when you go away.

Your reputation is learned in an hour;
Your character does not come to light for a year.

Reputation is made in a moment;
Character is built in a lifetime.

Reputation grows like a mushroom;
Character grows like an oak.

A single newspaper report gives you your reputation;
A life of toil gives you your character.

Reputation makes you rich or makes you poor;
Character makes you happy or makes you miserable.

Reputation is what men say about you on your tombstone;
Character is what angels say about you before the throne of God.

—William Hersey Davis[4]

5

Finding a Role Model, Part 1

How many graduation ceremonies have you already attended in your lifetime? I'm sure it's been quite a few, right?

Well, I wish I could have a graduation ceremony for you right this minute. Why? Because you have successfully completed an introduction to a very key step to studying the Bible—the process of observation, especially as it applies to narrative literature—and to you as a young woman.

So imagine me letting go of a bouquet of brightly colored helium-filled balloons, blowing a curly paper horn, and handing you a beautiful certificate with your name on it. Oh, and then there would be a big hug...and we would have to have a picture taken of us together...and then, of course, cake!

Moving On to Greater Growth

But, as the saying goes, "Graduation from one course of study is simply the beginning of the next step in learning." So now I invite you, dear graduate, to move on with me as we graduate to another type of literature found in the Bible—the wisdom literature. Understanding wisdom literature is yet another step toward growing into a woman after God's own heart as you unlock the wisdom God wants to pass on to you for your life today as well as for all your days to come.

This category of wisdom literature is found in the five books located in the middle of your Bible—books that are favorites for many Christians:

1. Job
2. Psalms
3. Proverbs
4. Ecclesiastes
5. Song of Songs

You may have heard these books of wisdom literature referred to as "the poetic books." Regardless of what we call them, these are the books that follow the NARRATIVE or historical books of the Bible (Genesis through Esther). From the stories in the historical books we now move on to poetry and pithy sayings!

~ BIBLE STUDY 101 ~
WISDOM LITERATURE

The wisdom books contain a completely different type of literature that speaks to the heart. They instruct your heart in ways to love and worship God, and praise and pray to God. Christians down through time have sought these books of the Bible in their times of suffering or confusion or when they needed to know the right thing to do and make a tough decision. Why, Song of Songs even tells a husband and wife how to love each other, while Ecclesiastes ponders the meaning of life.

Most of all, these wisdom books give you wisdom— just what you need to help you make the best daily choices and decisions! To get the most out of these poetic books, we will tackle two more steps in Bible study that will help you get to the bottom of poetic language and draw out its meaning.

~ BIBLE STUDY 101 ~
CROSS-REFERENCES

The next resource we want to use in Bible study is CROSS-REFERENCES. Cross-referencing Bible verses lets Scripture interpret Scripture. The reason it's vital for us to make use of cross-references is the fact that God does not contradict Himself. One portion of Scripture will never contradict another portion. Your goal is to understand each passage you are studying in light of the Bible's teaching as a whole. For the most part, whatever verse you are studying, the Bible contains other verses about that same topic or its meaning. The Bible is essentially one revelation, giving one consistent message about God and His will.

As you try to interpret what you read in the Bible, the first knowledge you need is finding out what God says about that same topic in other places. In your previous lessons about Esther, you learned about near context and far context. When it comes to cross-referencing, the primary principle to remember is that the whole

Bible is the ultimate context of every passage. Knowing what other passages say about a subject will help you understand what individual verses about the same subject mean or imply.

~ BIBLE STUDY 101 ~
CONSULTATION

After cross-referencing, the next step in studying your Bible is CONSULTATION. Previously you were asked to check out terms or words in a dictionary. Doing that is CONSULTATION: You consult outside sources or reference books like dictionaries, encyclopedias, maps, commentaries, and study Bibles to gain more insight into the meaning of the words used in your Bible. The act of CONSULTATION brings you closer to an accurate interpretation of the passage you are reading or studying, and guides you toward life-changing personal applications from the Word of God.

Ready, Set, Go!

As we move through the next few chapters in this book and take a closer look at "God's Ideal Woman," the woman portrayed in Proverbs 31, I'll give you some cross-references to look at and point you to some key words to look up in your dictionary. These exercises will cause your understanding of the Proverbs 31 woman to blossom and grow. As you move verse by verse through the 31 verses in Proverbs 31, you will not only be instructed by the verses, you'll also be challenged to become more and more like this woman who was so beautiful in God's eyes. Best of all, you will have a model—the ultimate model—for all of life, a model of what a godly woman looks like…and what she does and does not do.

Are you ready? Are you set? Then here we go! Grab your Bible, utter a prayer, and, as always, enjoy!

The Proverbs 31 Woman
Proverbs 31:1-9

> 1 The sayings of King Lemuel—an inspired utterance his mother taught him.

Who are the two people mentioned in this verse?

Person 1: _____

Person 2: _____

(A quick note: By looking in a Bible encyclopedia or Bible dictionary [CONSULTATION], you will discover that the name "Lemuel" means "dedicated to God" or "devoted to God.")

What is the man doing?

_____

_____

What is the woman doing?

_____

_____

Look at any dictionary (one you have at home, or online, or on your phone) and write out a definition of the word *taught* or *teach*.

_____

_____

_____

Read 2 Timothy 1:3-5. (This is a CROSS-REFERENCE to a teaching similar to Proverbs 31:1-2.) Who is the person addressed in these verses? (Hint: See the name of the book of the Bible. The apostle Paul is writing this "epistle" or letter to this man.)

_____

Who are the women named and referred to in 2 Timothy 1:5, and how are they related to the recipient of Paul's instruction?

_____

_____

What did Paul admire and point out about these two women?

_____

_____

Read 2 Timothy 3:14-15 (another CROSS-REFERENCE). Based on these verses, when did Timothy, Paul's right-hand man in ministry, learn the truths from the Bible?

_____

_____

What was the impact of the truths Timothy was taught at home?

_____

_____

Conclusion: Based on Proverbs 31:1, 2 Timothy 1:3-5, and 3:14-15, what is one key role God gives to mothers, and why is it so important?

_____

_____

_____

_____

Personal application: Do you have a mom who is trying to teach you truths from the Bible? Who encourages you to live by the Bible and have daily devotions or a quiet time? Who is making every effort to see that you know God's Word? If so,

— thank God for her, and
— thank her!

How about an attitude check? Do you make it hard or easy for your parents to talk about the things of God? To read together as a family from the Bible or a devotional book? To discuss spiritual things or the sermon you heard at church? Do you murmur? Complain? Whine? Sulk? Roll your eyes? Drag your heels? Clam up? Act like you are having to take some horrible medicine?

Here are some things to think about: Why would a young adult woman (that's you!) resist and resent a mother who is doing what the Bible says a godly mother should do? Why should a daughter "punish" her mom with a bad attitude when all she is doing is obeying God's instructions to her as a mother?

Join your parents' team. Do your part in absorbing the Word of God whenever it is put in front of you. Participate in the discussions that arise during devotions and family time. Show your younger siblings a good example of a learner, of what a person who loves God and His Word looks like, of a teen who respects her parents. And above all, pray that what your mom or parents are teaching you will accomplish what 2 Timothy 3:15 says—that it would "make you wise for salvation through faith in Christ Jesus."

More personal application: Wow! Can you believe all we've learned from just one verse, from Proverbs 31:1? By using your skills in OBSERVATION, CROSS-REFERENCES, CONSULTATION, and, of course, APPLICATION, you've learned life-changing principles from this verse! How has it changed your life? Or, what changes do you plan to make right away?

_____

_____

_____

_____

² Listen, my son! Listen, son of my womb! Listen,
my son, the answer to my prayers!

What words are repeated three times?

(verb) _____

(noun) _____

CONSULTATION: Write out the dictionary definition of the
word "listen."

_____

_____

_____

How does this mother describe the depth of her relationship to her son, her child?

  —

  —

Think about how this mother referred to her child, and the fact that his name means "dedicated to God" or "devoted to God." What does this tell you about her heart, love, feelings, passion, and emotions toward her son and toward her responsibility to teach him?

_____

_____

_____

_____

_____

Conclusion: Considering the intensity of the language this mother uses and the repetition of her heartfelt words, what can you conclude about what she is going to say to him? About the importance of the message she is getting ready to deliver to him?

_____

_____

_____

Personal application: How do you respond when one of your parents wants to tell you something? Do you listen—*really* listen? Do you stop what you are doing and turn toward them, watch their faces, stop thinking about what you are going to wear, or about how much you really don't want to hear what's coming, or how you really could use this time to finish your homework—and pay full attention? What changes do you need to make in your attitudes, heart, and actions?

_____

_____

_____

Also, coming from my heart as a mom, whether or not your mom expresses her love for you and your importance to her in the way this mom did, this kind of concern and these kinds of emotions are most definitely in her heart. You, dear daughter, are precious and priceless to your parents. As a baby, you were passionately wanted and eagerly anticipated. You are—and always will be—the subject of your parents' fervent prayers. Count on it, whether it's stated out loud or not. Not all mothers are as articulate as the poetry expressed in Proverbs 31:2, but their hearts are just as passionate.

> ³ Do not spend your strength on women, your vigor on those who ruin kings.

Here the mother's earnest instruction begins. Are you wondering why we are studying what a mom told her son, her boy? The answer is that she's moving toward verses 10-31, where she tells him what kind of woman to look for and marry! But first, she needs to instruct him in how to be a godly leader. After all, he would eventually become a king. So now we begin to hear her instructions on how to be a good king, instructions that are coming from a mother who some people say was probably married to a king.

What warning does the mother give to her son in verse 3?

_____

_____

_____

_____

What does she imply will happen if her son does not heed this warning?

_____

_____

CROSS-REFERENCE: Instead of spending time with many women, what does 1 Timothy 3:2 say a godly leader is to be and do?

_____

_____

Personal application: God's instruction here through Lemuel's mother is for godly guys to avoid temptation and avoid women who are not godly, women who could destroy their reputation and ruin their lives, women who can tempt them away from following God. So it follows that a godly woman, whatever her age, whether young or old, would be a woman who would do everything in her power to not tempt guys to sin in any way. What guidelines do these verses give you in the areas of purity and godliness?

1 Timothy 2:9 _____

Titus 2:5 _____

Personal application: What can you do to make sure you are not tempting boys by your behavior or dress? Or, put another way, what guidelines can you establish for your clothing and conduct?

_____

_____

_____

> [4] It is not for kings, Lemuel—it is not for kings to drink wine, not for rulers to crave beer,

After this mother covers the topic of women, what is the next topic she addresses?

_____

What phrase or phrases are used and repeated that makes this an extremely important message for this future leader and king?

_____

_____

CROSS-REFERENCE: What do these verses from Proverbs say are some of the effects of alcohol?

Proverbs 20:1—

Proverbs 21:17—

Proverbs 23:21—

CROSS-REFERENCE: Read Proverbs 23:29-35. This is a classic description of a drunkard and the effects alcohol has on the one who indulges in it. It is a sad picture of self-destruction. Every teen will one day be asked or tempted to drink alcohol. Do you have a plan for what you will do? What you will say? How you will handle the invitation? Proverbs is a book of wisdom, and wisdom always has a plan. So be prepared.

Most parents talk to their teen and preteen children about drinking and alcohol before they are presented with the temptation. If your parents haven't, why don't you ask them how you should respond when others tempt you to drink? You will be glad to know their thoughts and have their input. And you'll be glad to know you can talk with them openly about drinking.

> 5 lest they drink and forget what has been decreed, and deprive all the oppressed of their rights.

What does this wise mom tell her son could happen to him as a leader if he drinks too much?

—

—

CROSS-REFERENCE: Proverbs 31:5 refers to not forgetting "what has been decreed." When Moses died, Joshua was assigned by God to become Israel's new leader. What did God tell Joshua would help him to remember God's law, according to Joshua 1:8?

_____

_____

_____

CROSS-REFERENCE: Briefly summarize what Psalm 119:9-11 says will help you as a young person "to stay pure in a filthy environment."[1]

_____

_____

_____

_____

Personal application: What two or three things are you doing—or will you begin doing—to keep God's instructions fresh in your mind and heart?

1. _____

2. _____

3. _____

> ^{6} Let beer be for those who are perishing, wine
> for those who are in anguish! ^{7} Let them drink
> and forget their poverty and remember their mis-
> ery no more.

After telling her son twice that "it is not for kings" to drink
and crave alcohol, she then tells him who benefits from the
effects of alcohol.

Those who are perishing. CONSULTATION: How does the
dictionary define the word *perish*?

_____

_____

_____

Those who are in anguish. CONSULTATION: How does
the dictionary define the word *anguish*?

_____

_____

_____

According to verse 7, how would alcohol act like medicine
to help those who were suffering and dying?

_____

_____

_____

_____

8 Speak up for those who cannot speak for themselves, for the rights of all who are destitute. 9 Speak up and judge fairly; defend the rights of the poor and needy.

What words does this Proverbs 31 mother use twice while instructing her soon-to-be-a-leader son about his future role as a leader?

He must _____

What very important responsibilities of a person in leadership does Lemuel's mother stress?

_____

_____

_____

_____

_____

What kinds of people are especially to be defended, protected, and cared for by leaders and kings?

_____

_____

_____

_____

Primary application: Primary application is the application as it was meant in the actual text of the Scripture—what it means in context, applying the exact interpretation of the meaning of the truth presented. This means Proverbs 31:1-9 was first and foremost for the young man King Lemuel. These verses are specific instructions, from his mother to him, about a singular topic—how to be a godly king who judges and cares for his people according to God's law, how to be a godly king who curbs his lifestyle so he can rule according to God's law and represent those who are unable to defend themselves.

Personal application: You are not a man, and you are not a king, and you are probably not a political leader. However, like God's kings and like Jesus, who is the King of kings, you are to be compassionate and helpful and merciful to those who are suffering and in need. Share some ways you are currently reaching out to help others in need. Also, can you think of more ways you could come to the aid of those who need help?

_____

_____

_____

_____

How Can You Know What to Do... or Not Do?

Here are four questions to ask yourself that will help you answer the question above and others like it when you have to decide what you will or will not do:

1. Will it please God? Avoid anything that God will eventually judge and destroy.

2. Will it help me? Think about whether the activity is beneficial for your health and spiritual growth.

3. Could it enslave me? If the activity is tempting, addicting, or time-consuming, watch out.

4. Will it hurt someone else? Imagine what it would be like to be in that person's shoes.[2]

Looking at Your Life

Have you heard the expression, "A picture is worth a thousand words"? Well, that's exactly what God is giving you in Proverbs 31, a portion of poetic literature. This is God's picture of His kind of woman. And it begins with a woman—a passionate Proverbs 31 woman and mother—grooming and instructing her young son about his life as well as the kind of woman he should look for to marry. We'll dive into her description of an ideal and godly woman in our next chapter. But for now, recall and own these takeaway truths from verses 1-9 of Proverbs 31:

— Appreciate and pay attention when your mom or dad gives you guidance about the best way to live your life.

— Become a lifelong learner who seeks, listens to, and values godly advice and wise counsel.

— Set your standards now about what you will and will not do based on God's Word.

— Stay pure and on track with God by taking in His Word and arming yourself spiritually day by day.

— Be a blessing to others by being compassionate, merciful, and helpful.

6

Finding a Role Model, Part 2

I'm sure you've probably had this experience. You're watching a favorite TV series and, just as you've invested almost an hour in the current episode…you get to the end and see the words, "To Be Continued."

Well, this chapter continues from the previous chapter. To illustrate the thrill of discovering and understanding the meaning of God's Word, I've chosen for us to make our way together through the entire chapter of Proverbs 31. I selected it because it contains a l-o-t of pink scriptures that will shape your life forever as a woman. And it's taught by a woman who serves as a powerful model of what a woman after God's own heart looks like and does—how she lives her life.

To recap (as in the "Previously seen on this program" lead-ins on the plot from a previous episode), previously we met a truly godly woman in the mother of a young son. And she's passionately teaching him and shaping and preparing him for his future. She herself is dedicated and devoted to God and, as her son Lemuel's name means ("dedicated to God" or "devoted to God"), she has dedicated and devoted her son to God too.

Covering All the Bases

In Proverbs 31:1-9 this mother spoke about the character qualities and habits that should mark out a king and a leader and a godly man. Then beginning in verse 10, she offers 22 sayings to help her son find an "ideal wife." She creates an alphabetical list of qualities that a suitable wife would possess. And, if you like puzzles, you'll be interested to know these 22 verses were originally written in the Hebrew language, and the Hebrew alphabet is made up of 22 letters. So she begins each verse, or proverb, or character quality with a letter of the alphabet. That makes Proverbs 31:10-31 an alphabetical acrostic.

Maybe this mother's son was young enough that the use of the alphabet, like the ABCs, would help make her advice easier to remember. Whatever her reason for using an acrostic, it worked, because Proverbs 31 is King Lemuel passing on the "utterance his mother taught him" (see verse 1).

Bonus question: Before we start on the ABCs from the Hebrew alphabet in Proverbs 31:10-31, take a look at several other Bible passages that are alphabetical as well. As you quickly scan them, jot down anything that catches your attention or speaks to your heart or is noted in your Bible.

Psalm 25—

Psalm 34—

Psalm 119—

Lamentations 3 (Hint: Divide the total number of verses that make up Lamentations chapter 3 by 22, the number of letters of the Hebrew alphabet)—

Learning God's ABCs

When I speak at conferences on Proverbs 31:10-31, I use the English alphabet as I teach through these 22 verses. Because this makes the meaning of each verse easier to comprehend and remember, I'll give you my alphabet at the end of this chapter and the next. As we begin making our way through this life-changing and life-shaping material, pause, ask God to open your eyes and your heart to His truths. Then thank Him for this feminine model who will serve you for a lifetime!

> Verse 10: A wife of noble character who can find?
> She is worth far more than rubies.

What kind of woman is most important to find?

_____

How valuable and how much is such a woman worth?

_____

CONSULTATION: Bible reference books reveal that the Hebrew word translated "noble" or "virtuous" or "excellent" is used some 200-plus times in the Bible to describe an army of men, men of war, and men prepared for war.

CONSULTATION: A Bible dictionary gives us definitions that help us understand the meaning of the word "noble" in Proverbs 31:10 and elsewhere. This Old Testament word refers to a "force" and is used to mean "able, capable, mighty, strong, valiant, powerful, efficient, wealthy," and "worthy."[1] Its primary meaning refers to military strength.

CROSS-REFERENCE: According to the Bible passages below, what kinds of men were considered noble?

Exodus 18:25 _____

_____

Joshua 1:14 _____

_____

Joshua 6:2-3 _____

_____

Ruth 2:1 _____

_____

1 Samuel 9:1 _____

_____

1 Chronicles 12:25 _____

_____

CONCLUSION: Just as the two forces of mental toughness and physical energy are primary traits of soldiers in an army, they also mark God's Proverbs 31 woman. Four, and only four, scriptures in the Bible use the Hebrew word translated "noble" to describe a woman or women. You've already observed Proverbs 31:10. Now look at the other three.

Ruth 3:11—What did the man Boaz say about Ruth?

_____

_____

Proverbs 12:4—How is the excellent woman of Proverbs 12:4 described?

_____

_____

Proverbs 31:29—What accolade does the husband of this woman give to his wife?

_____

_____

CONSULTATION: Bible reference books inform us that different translations of Proverbs 31:10 use different words to describe what a treasure this woman is. Some use "rubies." Some use "coral." And some use "pearls." Whatever the translation—and whatever the jewel—each was considered a priceless treasure. And our lady is worth "far more" than rubies, or coral, or pearls!

What a wealth of information we have as we head into the specifics of what makes the Proverbs 31 woman so remarkable, and in only 15 words! Our CONCLUSION? Our model is priceless, a noble, excellent, virtuous woman of character, rare and more valuable than all the treasure in the world. She is *an army of virtues.*

INTERPRETATION: What kind of picture do these definitions paint of a woman of noble or excellent character? Complete this sentence with your own words: A woman of noble character is not a wimp or an emotional wreck: She is a woman who is

_____

_____

_____

Personal application: As a woman who is totally used to looking into mirrors all day long, do as James 1:22-25 advises and peer into the mirror of God's Word. In light of what you've learned about the meaning of Proverbs 31:10, what two or three changes should—and will—you make right away to strengthen your character qualities so you can be on track to becoming a more excellent and awesome woman?

I need to stop/start...

_____

_____

I need to stop/start...

_____

_____

I need to stop/start...

_____

_____

Verse 11: Her husband has full confidence in her
and lacks nothing of value.

Because of this woman's many character qualities, what
are two blessings her husband enjoys?

—

—

Verse 12: She brings him good, not harm, all the
days of her life.

How else does this excellent woman and wife bless her husband?

_____

What does she not bring or cause her husband?

_____

For how long?

_____

Personal application: As a young woman who isn't married, don't forget that the quality we are admiring here in the Proverbs 31 woman is her faithfulness. How do you measure up on the faithfulness scale? Or put another way, how would those who know you best—your family, your friends, your schoolmates, and teammates—rate you when it comes to your faithfulness and your work ethic, and why?

_____

_____

_____

If you have uncovered a few gaps and flaws, make immediate plans to do something about them. As James 1:25 promises, those who look intently at the teachings of the Word of God and do it—"they will be blessed in what they do."

> Verse 13: She selects wool and flax and works with eager hands.

CULTURE: When you study the Bible, you should make a note of when the book of the Bible you are studying was written, when the events occurred in history. The book of Proverbs was written almost 3000 years ago. According to verse 13, what kinds of work during her day and age does the Proverbs 31 woman participate in?

_____

_____

What do you learn about her work ethic?

_____

_____

Personal application and attitude check—How do you respond to the work you have to do—your schoolwork, your homework, your chores? When Mom asks you to do something or help out with your brother or sister, how do you respond? Is it, "Oh, no! Why me? Do I have to do it right now? Oh, a-l-l right!"?

It's a fact of life: There are many things we must do each day. Most of them we have no power over—we simply must do them. But your attitude toward your work is always your choice. CROSS-REFERENCE: Write out Colossians 3:23. Then write it out on an index card and carry it with you.

_____

_____

_____

_____

According to this verse, what is a key to doing any and all your work with a happy heart?

_____

_____

14 She is like the merchant ships, bringing her food from afar.

Oh joy—shopping trip! How is the Proverbs 31 woman described in this verse?

_____

NEAR CONTEXT: According to verse 13, what did she seek for making clothing?

_____

In verse 14, what is she seeking?

_____

CROSS-REFERENCE and CULTURE: For an exciting glimpse of the "merchant ships," read 2 Chronicles 9:21 and notice some of the unique items they carried from port to port. Check here when you are done. _____

Think about God's imagery and description of the Proverbs 31 lady "sailing" through her daily errands. What do you think "puts the wind in her sails" as she runs to and fro to gather up goods?

_____

_____

Personal application: Make a list of your daily duties and responsibilities. Do you have to watch over or transport a younger brother or sister? Do you have to help with dinner or cleanup? Do you have to practice on an instrument? Take care of your clothes? And of course, there's your schoolwork.

_____

_____

_____

As you look at your duties and responsibilities and your heart attitude and your conduct toward them, what is your general day-by-day attitude? Please be honest.

_____

_____

_____

Write out a plan or steps you will take to own and accept your responsibilities, to approach them with the energy and joy and commitment the Proverbs 31 woman models for you.

_____

_____

_____

15 She gets up while it is still night; she provides food for her family and portions for her female servants.

What do you learn about this woman's personal daily schedule?

_____

_____

What was one of her reasons for this daily habit?

_____

_____

Who were the recipients of her early morning work?

_____

_____

CONSULTATION and CULTURE: A look at a reference book on Bible customs reveals that "portions" not only meant food for the day, but also instructions of tasks and work assignments for the day.

Personal application: What do you think would happen if you got up just a little earlier each day? What could you get done that you should do and that you want to do? Make a list and try getting up earlier every day for a week. Don't forget to journal all the wonderful things you accomplish and the progress you make.

_____

_____

_____

[16] She considers a field and buys it; out of her earnings she plants a vineyard.

There is no end to this lady's energy! As she takes care of her home and the people who live in it, what is her next step for their food provisions?

_____

_____

How did she finance her ventures?

_____

_____

CONSULTATION: Here's a key word concerning this woman's character—she "considers" a field. Using your dictionary, write out the definition of the verb "consider."

_____

_____

_____

Personal application: What can you learn—and change—from the Proverbs 31 gal about making wise decisions?

_____

_____

_____

¹⁷ She sets about her work vigorously; her arms are strong for her tasks.

CROSS-REFERENCE: What did you learn about this woman's work ethic in verse 13?

_____

_____

What additional information do you find about her work ethic and her *mental energy* here in verse 17?

_____

_____

What do you also learn about her *physical energy* and condition?

_____

_____

CROSS-REFERENCE: Use your Bible to look up the verses that follow. What resources are available to motivate you as you approach your work and projects?

Nehemiah 8:10—

Philippians 4:13—

Personal application: What one thing will you do this week to adjust your mental attitude toward your work and responsibilities?

_____

_____

_____

What one thing will you do this week to increase your physical energy? Do you need more sleep? Do you need to engage in some kind of physical activity? Do you need to change your diet and eat foods that give you healthy energy and stamina and give up the foods that bring you down, that make you want to take a nap? Think about it and write down your one thing.

_____

_____

_____

P.S. What should be your goal in the energy department according to our woman's conduct—and goal—in Proverbs 31:27?

_____

_____

18 She sees that her trading is profitable, and her lamp does not go out at night.

What result does our Proverbs 31 woman realize from her hard work and diligent efforts?

_____

_____

_____

CROSS-REFERENCE: What do these verses in Proverbs 31 tell you this woman created, sold, and traded that brought in means to help support her family?

Verse 13—

Verse 16—

Verse 24—

Because our Proverbs 31 friend realized financial benefits from her skills, hobbies, talents, hard work, and efforts,
what decision did she make regarding her time?

_____

_____

Personal application: What is your favorite hobby? Are you
into crafts? Photography? Art? Has God blessed you with a talent? Jot down several answers here.

_____

_____

_____

_____

List a few things you can do or change to create more time
to work on something you love doing. What can you stop
doing, and what can you start doing?

_____

_____

_____

_____

[19] In her hand she holds the distaff and grasps
the spindle with her fingers.

NEAR CONTEXT: What did you learn from verse 18 about
our lady's evenings?

_____

_____

Verse 19 reveals what she may have been doing in the evenings. Write the answer here.

_____

_____

CONSULTATION: Using your dictionary, give a brief definition of:

distaff—

spindle—

CONCLUSION: What do you conclude she was doing
when she stayed up just a little longer in the evenings?

_____

_____

^{20} She opens her arms to the poor and extends
her hands to the needy.

God's excellent woman of character was a hard worker, highly motivated, diligent, and kept her eye on the financial well-being of her family. She not only managed household assets, but contributed to them as well. Now, in verse 20, we see a softer set of character qualities in her, and we get a glimpse into what she did with some of her hard-earned assets. What two things do you see her doing?

—

—

CROSS-REFERENCE: In a few words, what do these scriptures say we should have at the core of our hearts?

Deuteronomy 15:7-8—

Proverbs 11:25—

Proverbs 19:17—

Proverbs 22:9—

Micah 6:8—

CROSS-REFERENCE: Take a quick look at another woman of character in 2 Kings 4:8-11. Who had a need?

_____

Many have needs, but not all notice them. Who noticed the need in this setting?

_____

Many notice someone has a need, but not all act on it. What did this noble woman do about the need she noticed?

_____

_____

Personal application: Our lessons on the Proverbs 31 woman are, once again, "To be continued." But before you go, take time to pray right now and ask God to give you eyes that see and ears that hear—and a heart that is moved to act when someone is in need.

Earlier I mentioned that whenever I teach on the Proverbs 31 woman, I use the English alphabet to help make the meaning of each verse easier to comprehend and remember. Here's the first half of that alphabet—which lists what we covered in this chapter:

The ABCs of Godly Character

1. 31:10—She is an **A**rmy
2. 31:11—She is a **B**lessing
3. 31:12—She is **C**onsiderate
4. 31:13—She is **D**iligent
5. 31:14—She is **E**nterprising
6. 31:15—She is **F**aithful
7. 31:16—She is a **G**ardener
8. 31:17—She is **H**earty
9. 31:18—She is **I**ndustrious
10. 31:19—She has a **J**ob at night
11. 31:20—She is **K**ind

Looking at Your Life

Proverbs 31:10-31 is a look at the daily life and character qualities modeled by God's ideal and excellent woman. It's true she lived about 3000 years ago, but the Word of the Lord stands forever. It is the counsel of His heart to all generations. And it will never change (Isaiah 40:8). The same character qualities that make our "P31 Woman" so beautiful in God's eyes are the ones that will give you true beauty too.

So please, make the most of the personal application sections and put God's wisdom to work in your life—today. Apply it right now! You will be preparing yourself for your future, whether you marry or not.

Our primary goal in discovering the riches of Proverbs 31 is to gain a good understanding of what character traits and virtues are important to God, to you, and to the people your life touches and blesses. Above all, this is a key passage for every Christian woman, young or old, single or married. It is filled with wisdom that will help you as a woman through every day of your life.

7

Finding a Role Model, Part 3

I hope you are falling in love with the pithy teaching style—and the wisdom—of the book of Proverbs. And especially the incredible woman brought to life in Proverbs 31! We'll see some additional proverbs in chapters to come, but for now, there's more to learn from God's excellent model for His women of all ages and stages.

I receive a lot of mail! And I have to say that the Number One question I'm asked is this: "Where are the older women who are mentioned in Titus 2?" Women around the world are wondering, "Where are the women who are supposed to mentor and guide me? Where are the women who are supposed to model Christian conduct and priorities for me?"

From Day One as a baby Christian, at age 28, I began looking for a role model. What I was reading in my new Bible was wonderful! I wanted everything I was reading—especially what I was marking with my pink highlighter pen. Pink was the color I had designated for marking passages in the Bible that talked about women, wives, mothers, and the role and ministry of women in the church.

Well, all I can say is, "Praise God for the Proverbs 31 woman!" She shows you and me not only *what* we are to do to be godly women, but *how* we are to do it. Do you ever wonder what your priorities should be? Well, this lady tells you and models it for you. She lives it.

My friend, in God's photo album of the remarkable Proverbs 31 woman you will find instruction, encouragement, a model to follow, and the motivation to keep you looking to God and living for Him for a lifetime. And most important of all, you'll find out about true beauty—God's kind of beauty.

Like yummy, refreshing ice cream, let's go for another scoop. Even another bowlful! Let's enjoy more of Ms. P31's energy, productivity, focus, and accomplishments. And let's see how her story ends.

Proverbs 31:21-31

21 When it snows, she has no fear for her household; for all of them are clothed in scarlet.

What kind of preparations did this Proverbs 31 lady make for her family?

_____

_____

How did her preparations and forward planning pay off for her emotionally?

_____

_____

NEAR CONTEXT and CROSS-REFERENCE: Revisit these verses in Proverbs 31 and note her other farsighted preparations:

Verse 15—

Verse 27—

CROSS-REFERENCE: What do these proverbs (found outside of Proverbs 31) teach you about the wisdom of preparation?

Proverbs 6:6-8—

Proverbs 10:5—

Proverbs 27:23-27—

Personal application: The Bible makes it clear in many places that you are not to worry or be anxious. But, as you are seeing here in Proverbs, it is just as clear that you should be actively preparing for future events, projects, deadlines, and possible needs and disasters. What's on your schedule? Got any papers due? Any exams coming up? Are you going to audition for a special activity? Do you need to study for your driver's license test? Will you be taking your SAT exam soon? Name your upcoming challenge or responsibility—or dream.

What steps and actions do you need to take to be prepared and ready for your challenge? Make some initial notes here, but do your detailed planning on your calendar or in a personal notebook or phone app.

_____

_____

_____

22 She makes coverings for her bed; she is clothed in fine linen and purple.

Our lady is busy—and creative! In addition to coats and cloaks of wool, what else did she make...

...for her home?

...for herself?

CONSULTATION and CULTURE: Looking into reference materials reveals that "fine linen" glistens like silk, and anything "purple" was colored by a rare and costly dye that had probably arrived on the merchant ships.

NEAR CONTEXT: Quickly look at the verses on the next page. They are all from Proverbs 31. Jot down a brief description of our lady's activities.

Verse 13—

Verse 19—

Verse 22—

Verse 24—

As you think about these facts, what do they tell you about the Proverbs 31 woman's...

...skills?

...abilities?

...use of time?

...attitude toward her home?

...heart?

What is your "thing"? Your passion? What are your hobbies? What skills and abilities do you possess? Jot down the first or strongest or favorite one that pops into your mind.

My "thing" is _____

How can you fit in more time to develop the talent God has given you? Be prepared: You may have to give something else up to gain the time you need to improve and master your talent.

The first step (or two) I will take to improve my skill is:

_____

_____

_____

23 Her husband is respected at the city gate, where he takes his seat among the elders of the land.

At last we learn more about Mr. Proverbs 31! OBSERVA-TION: What place is mentioned?

_____

What do you learn about his character?

_____

What is his position and service in the community, and who are his colleagues?

_____

CULTURE and CROSS-REFERENCE: In the days of the Proverbs 31 woman, cities were surrounded by walls for protection. Gated entrances containing large rooms were built into the city wall. The "elders" were the members of the judicial body who ruled the land. This prestigious group met daily in the town gate to transact any public business or decide cases that were brought before them. What are some of the activities that went on in "the gates" according to these verses?

Ruth 4:1-5—

2 Samuel 15:1-2—

Esther 2:21-23—

What can you surmise about this husband's "job" or his role in the community?

A personal note: In my book on Proverbs 31, *Beautiful in God's Eyes for Young Women*, I wrote these words about this husband and wife team: "He exerts his influence on the life of the community in the city gates; she influences the community from home."[1] Both are involved and committed to their community and its people, yet each makes their contribution in their own sphere of influence.

> [24] She makes linen garments and sells them, and
> supplies the merchants with sashes.

Meet the businesswoman side of the Proverbs 31 woman! What does she make, and what does she do with her products?

_____

_____

Do you have an avenue for earning money? Do you babysit? Can you walk and care for pets? Make jewelry? Do computer work or artwork or video editing? Check with your parents before you do anything, but start thinking about what you are good at, what you love doing, and how you could help others out and earn a little money for your expenses, gift giving, church camp, hobbies, uniforms, you name it!

_____

_____

_____

²⁵ She is clothed with strength and dignity; she can laugh at the days to come.

You've heard it before: It's what's inside that counts. We've seen our gal's clothing—and know it's gorgeous and magnificent. But what do you learn from this verse about her inner wear—her character?

_____

_____

How does her inner character affect her outlook on life?

_____

_____

Instead of worrying about the future, what is her response?

_____

CROSS-REFERENCE: Other translations of Proverbs 31:25 read:

She shall rejoice in time to come (NKJV).

She smiles at the future (NASB).

She laugheth at the time to come (ASV).

As author Anne Ortlund shares, this woman's ability to smile and laugh at her future "puts the lines on her face in the right places."[2] As you look down through the corridor of time future, what are your thoughts? Dreams? Fears? Questions? Desires? What is the one response that most often pops up?

_____

How does the Proverbs 31 woman's outlook on the future encourage you and challenge you?

_____

_____

_____

To help you keep your eye and mind on today and have a positive attitude about each precious day God gives you to live for Him, I've included a page at the end of this chapter entitled "An Invitation to Beauty" (see page 143). Copy it. Give it to all your friends—and your mom! But most of all, live it!

> 26 She speaks with wisdom, and faithful instruction is on her tongue.

What woman doesn't have problems with what she says?! However, our P31 woman set two rules for content for her mouth. What are they?

—

—

CROSS-REFERENCE: Which use of her mouth and words did you observe in Proverbs 31:1-9?

_____

The book of Proverbs has much to say about the mouth and your speech—your choice of words. To gain more wisdom about your speech and what to say and not say, quickly look at the following verses from Proverbs and write out the words of each verse.

Your Mouth

Proverbs 10:11—The mouth of the righteous is

_____

_____ .

Proverbs 10:31—From the mouth of the righteous

_____

_____

_____ .

Proverbs 11:13—A gossip _____ ,

but a trustworthy person _____ .

Proverbs 17:28—Even fools are thought wise if

_____ ,

and discerning if they _____

_____ .

Your Words

Proverbs 10:19—Sin is not ended by _____ ,

but the prudent _____

_____ .

Proverbs 12:18—

_____

_____

_____

Proverbs 15:1—

_____

_____

_____

Proverbs 15:23—

_____

_____

_____

Proverbs 16:21—

_____

_____

_____

Proverbs 16:23-24—

_____

_____

_____

Scan through these new principles for speech and put a check mark by the three you want to apply right away.

CROSS-REFERENCE: Three women in the Bible (mine are marked with pink, of course!) show us how they used their mouths in a good (if not the best) way. What happened when they opened their mouths?

Mary in Luke 1:46-47—

Anna in Luke 2:38—

The older women in Titus 2:3-4—

Bonus question: Hannah shows us the best thing to do when others are mean. Read 1 Samuel 1:1-10. When her life seemed to be caving in, how did she use her mouth in verse 10?

_____

> 27 She watches over the affairs of her household
> and does not eat the bread of idleness.

Looking at this verse, write out:

Lesson 1: _____

_____

Lesson 2: _____

_____

Your "household" is your space. Whether you have your own room or share it with a sister, you can and should "watch over" your portion of the space. Beyond that there is extended space that includes the house or dorm room or apartment where you live and which you share with others. Here are a few "rules to live by" that will help you to watch over your place and your extended place.

> If you open it, close it.
> If you turn it on, turn it off.
> If you unlock it, lock it up.
> If you break it, admit it.
> If you can't fix it, call in someone who can.
> If you borrow it, return it.
> If you value it, take care of it.
> If you make a mess, clean it up.

> If you move it, put it back.
> If it belongs to someone else,
>   get permission to use it.[3]

Think about your responsibilities. Your parents have probably given you chores to do at home. You have your schoolwork on top of life at home. Maybe you have a part-time job. And if you are in a Bible study, or are a member of a team or play an instrument, you have commitments to keep up with. Are you wondering, "How can I get everything done? How in the world can I take care of all my responsibilities?"

Lesson 2 of Proverbs 31:27 has a huge answer for you. Write it out again and put it to work now! You will definitely see results.

_____

_____

[28] Her children arise and call her blessed; her husband also, and he praises her.

Here's a great use of your mouth and words! What did the children of the Proverbs 31 woman do with their mouths and words?

_____

_____

CONSULTATION and CULTURE: A look into a few Bible reference books will tell you a little something about the meaning of "arise." It can literally mean rising up and standing up, or it can figuratively mean growing up and going on to live in a way that honors the mother. Either way, these children are paying tribute to their mother.

God's instruction here in Proverbs 31:28 is a life assignment for you as a daughter: Be a blessing to your parents. Honor them, do what they say, and make sure you contribute positively to the atmosphere at home—instead of being a troublemaker and the source of contention and arguments.

Jot down a step you will take today—right now, if you can—to honor your mom. How hard is it to simply say, "I love you, Mom. Thanks for all you do. You're the best!" Say it, mean it, and make it a daily habit.

Looking back at verse 28—what did the husband of the Proverbs 31 woman do and say?

---

²⁹ Many women do noble things, but you surpass them all.

NEAR CONTEXT: Look again at verse 28. Who is saying these words spoken in verse 29?

And to whom is he speaking?

_____

NEAR CONTEXT: There are many who think that living as the Proverbs 31 woman did is unattainable. I've heard lots of women say they've simply given up because they think it is impossible to attain this level of excellence. But no. OBSERVATION shows us the opposite. Verse 29 tells us that "many" are noble. "Many" are excellent. "Many" achieve this level seen in the Proverbs 31 woman's life. It just so happens that, in the eyes of her children and husband, this woman, wife, and mom surpasses them all.

Quickly look again at page 102 in this book at the definitions of the meaning of "noble" as used in the Bible. I'm thinking that by the time you are finishing up this current chapter you've made some changes in your life that are moving you into God's "noble category" of females. How thrilling! Please jot down one or two changes God has worked in your heart—and pause to thank Him with all your heart!

1. _____

_____

2. _____

_____

A Prayer to Pray

Thank You, God, for these changes which, by Your grace, have recently occurred in my life. Help me to remain faithful—and to continue to grow into the woman You want me to be. Amen.

30 Charm is deceptive, and beauty is fleeting; but a woman who fears the Lᴏʀᴅ is to be praised.

It's easy to focus on outward beauty. In fact, it may be impossible *not* to focus on outward beauty. After all, you have to look at yourself in the mirror every day, even many times during every day! But here in Proverbs 31:30 God gives us a Bottom-Line Beauty Tip: A woman who fears the Lord is to be praised.

What does God—and the mother who is teaching this information to her son—say about:

Charm? _____

Definition: _____

Beauty? _____

Definition: _____

Use a dictionary to define these two terms.

What accounts for this woman's real beauty?

_____

CONSULTATION: As the writer of one Bible commentary on the book of Proverbs noted of the woman being described,

"Verse 30 is the capstone of this woman's noble character. She may be charming as well as beautiful, but her real beauty rests in her total commitment to God. Praise befits such a woman 'who fears the LORD.'"[4]

Here's a question: How much time do you spend each day making sure you look good on the outside? How does that compare to the amount of time you spend each day in God's Word tending your inner beauty? Be sure to make any needed adjustments in this ratio.

> [31] Honor her for all that her hands have done,
>   and let her works bring her praise at the city gate.

Look again at Proverbs 31:10 and write out the question asked there.

_____

_____

As we end our study of Proverbs 31, it's obvious with verse 31 that we've found one—we have found such a woman! We have come full circle. Verse 10 began by pointing to an ideal woman, a noble woman, and asks whether anyone could ever find one. Then as we moved verse by verse, we saw an impressive list of character qualities, attitudes, actions, and priorities—a list that grew longer and longer as God described and defined a woman who, whatever her age, is virtuous, noble, godly, excellent…and so on.

We now know that the Proverbs 31 woman influenced her family and community from her home. We've seen how she quietly went about the business of securing what her family needed, even designing and creating their clothing and home furnishings. We know she cared for the needy. We spotted her at work in her field. And—if this is the same woman from verses 1-9, as a godly mother, she faithfully instructed her child or children in what it means to fear the Lord, to live for Him, and follow Him with a whole heart.

According to the first half of verse 31, what does such a woman deserve?

_____

What are you and all others instructed to do?

_____

_____

I repeat, we now know that the Proverbs 31 woman influenced her family and community from her home. But what do you learn in the second half of verse 31?

_____

_____

OBSERVATION: Are any places or locations mentioned? If so, what places?

_____

CROSS-REFERENCE: Just for fun, look again at verse 23. What do 23 and 31 say about the positive influence and ministry a couple after God's own heart can have on their community?

The ABCs of Godly Character

Now that we have reached the end of our time with Ms. Proverbs 31, it's time to look again at our alphabet. Only this time, let's look at all the letters together!

1. 31:10—She is an **A**rmy
2. 31:11—She is a **B**lessing
3. 31:12—She is **C**onsiderate
4. 31:13—She is **D**iligent
5. 31:14—She is **E**nterprising
6. 31:15—She is **F**aithful
7. 31:16—She is a **G**ardener
8. 31:17—She is **H**earty
9. 31:18—She is **I**ndustrious
10. 31:19—She has a **J**ob at night
11. 31:20—She is **K**ind
12. 31:21—She **L**ooks to the future
13. 31:22—She is **M**agnificently clothed
14. 31:23—She is a **N**oble wife
15. 31:24—She is an **O**utstanding professional
16. 31:25—She is **P**repared for the future
17. 31:26—She speaks in a **Q**uiet manner

18. 31:27—She **R**uns her household

19. 31:28—She has **S**tars in her crown

20. 31:29—She is **T**ruly outstanding

21. 31:30—She has **U**nusual beauty

22. 31:31—She enjoys **V**oices of praise

Looking at Your Life

The last three chapters are entitled "Finding a Role Model." As the expression states, "A picture is worth a thousand words." And that's exactly what God is giving you in Proverbs 31, a portion of poetic literature. This is God's picture of His kind of woman and the kind of woman He wants you to be. The woman of Proverbs 31 is God's portrait of a woman of excellence…a woman you can become day by day and in the future.

Unfortunately, the world around you presents an entirely different kind of model for you to follow. Both Satan and today's culture have rejected God's ideal as described in Proverbs 31 and labeled it as being undesirable, old-fashioned, and behind the times. Don't do what Eve did and fall for the lies of the enemy and modern society. Please, oh please, follow God's model found in Proverbs 31. After all, she *is* His ideal woman.

Give her the honor God asks for in verse 31. Better yet, honor her by following and mimicking her as God's model of true feminine beauty.

An Invitation to Beauty

Hopefully you can see how each of these areas in your life can be strengthened so that, like the beautiful woman in Proverbs 31, you can rejoice in each day and in the future. Here are a few "just for today" thoughts:

Just for today...
> give your life afresh to God.

Just for today...
> show love to your family and be "too nice."

Just for today...
> think about how you use your money.

Just for today...
> pay attention to what you eat and drink.

Just for today...
> grow in character through the choices you make.

Just for today...
> reach out and encourage your best friend in her spiritual journey.

Just for today...
> utter a prayer to God to wake up tomorrow and repeat this plan for your inner beauty.[5]

8

Following After God's Own Heart

I absolutely love writing books to help women of all ages. One reason for this passion is the fact that I had to start learning from ground zero—at age 28!—how to be a woman, wife, and mom after God's own heart. I knew I was failing in every area of my life, and God's Word came to my rescue with answers for me—*all* of the answers. My early days of reading and discovering the truths in my cherished Bible were a dream come true! My entire life boiled down to my need to know two things: What does the Bible say I need to do? And, how do I do it?

In every book I write, my goal and purpose is to share from the Scriptures to help us as women with our daily life issues. It's been my joy and privilege to write a number of books, including *A Young Woman After God's Own Heart,*[1] that focus on what it means to follow God. He intends for us to follow Him and grow as Christians. It is His desire that we grow in our knowledge of Him and love for Him. Jesus asked His followers—including you and me—to "Follow Me." Read on.

What Does It Mean to Follow Jesus?

In Matthew 4:18-20, Jesus was just beginning His ministry, and He was looking for people He could train to take His message of salvation to a lost world. In the midst of His search, here's what happened:

> 18 As Jesus was walking beside the Sea of Galilee, he saw two brothers, Simon called Peter and his brother Andrew. They were casting a net into the lake, for they were fishermen.
>
> 19 "Come, follow me," Jesus said, "and I will send you out to fish for people."
>
> 20 At once they left their nets and followed him.

What was Jesus' command or call to the two fishermen in verse 19?

_____

_____

What was their response to Jesus' call (verse 20)?

_____

_____

Jesus asked for a commitment from these men, but they didn't have to respond. And yet they did! They chose to follow Jesus. And that's what Jesus wants from you too. He wants you to desire to follow Him wholeheartedly—not reluctantly with kicking and screaming all the way, but willingly and with great joy. What does a desire to follow Jesus look like? It means you want to grow spiritually. And to do this means you will need to make a few important decisions.

1. *Choose to read your Bible.* Why? This is where you meet with God. As you read His Word, He speaks to you through what you are reading. God isn't going to make you spend time with Him. No, this is your decision. Jesus' disciples often retreated to be with Him and be refreshed and encouraged by Him. That's what happens to you when you choose to spend time hearing Him through the Scriptures.

You're probably thinking, *Where will I find time to spend with God? After all, I'm already very busy!* Well, think about this: How much time do you spend on social media, on texting and talking on the phone with your friends, watching TV, wandering through the mall with your friends? Why not take some of that time and choose to spend it with God? For instance, how much time could you spend reading your Bible tomorrow? Make it an appointment—and do it. I guarantee you will be blessed! James 4:8 invites you to "Come near to God and he will come near to you."

2. *Choose to talk to God.* Any relationship requires that both parties communicate with each other. God speaks to you through His Word, the Bible, and you speak to God through your prayers. Now don't freak out over the idea of prayer! It's nothing more than talking to God. You talk to your girl-friends, don't you, and probably a l-o-t? Well, God wants to be your friend too—your best friend. He wants to help you make the right kinds of choices. So why not talk to Him and ask for His advice and help? As the Lord said, "Call to me and I will answer you"—and then He adds this bonus—"and tell

you great and unsearchable things you do not know" (Jeremiah 33:3). Wow!

3. *Choose to confess sin.* How can you follow Jesus if you let sin go unchecked? You know that Jesus died to take away the penalty of sin, which is death. But there are still the daily sins that you and I commit that hinder our relationship with Jesus.

Confession is admitting what you have done that is against God's will. The act of confession restores your relationship with God and allows the Holy Spirit to again flow freely through you to help you live for Jesus. Write out 1 John 1:9, which explains what happens in confession:

_____

_____

_____

4. *Choose to make some sacrifices.* Any truly great endeavor demands some sacrifice. Nothing of any substance happens without effort. The Christian life is one of willing sacrifice and commitment. It's no different than joining a sports team, or taking gymnastic lessons or music lessons. You join and are expected to make some sacrifices—actually, a lot of sacrifices! Well, God is asking for you to follow Him with all your heart—to make the same kind of commitment.

So what activities would you be willing to scale back or give up in order to gain something greater—in order to grow in your spiritual life? Check an area in which you are willing to cut back so you can focus more on living for God:

_____ Say no to some time watching TV or checking and posting on social media.

_____ Say no to some time with friends.

_____ Say no to some time on the phone.

_____ Say no to something else, like _____.

Jesus said, "If anyone wishes to come after Me, he must deny himself, and take up his cross and follow Me" (Matthew 16:24 NASB). Are you ready to make a more serious commitment to following Jesus? If you are, then you'll be well on your way to being a woman who follows after God's own heart.

~ BIBLE STUDY 101 ~

While you continue to move forward in understanding how to study your Bible, we want to continue working through another thrilling narrative passage in God's Word. Earlier in this book we learned about the first step in Bible study—OBSERVATION. We'll continue learning the principles of observation in this chapter as well. The key elements of observation are to ask and answer the kinds of questions that appear below. As you review, you'll find some additional information you can look for, clues that will help you dig out and collect the treasures of truth contained in the Bible.

WHO are the people? If a pronoun such as *he* or *she* or *they* is used, read backward to find the people's names. How are they described? Is any information given regarding their lineage?

WHAT did the people do? Or, WHAT's happening? Is someone teaching? If so, what—and what was the effect of the teaching? Is it a miracle? If so, what happened? Is it a battle? An argument or a debate? If so, who's winning? Is it a travelogue? If so, who's going where...and why?

WHERE did this event or scene take place? Is a country, area, or town mentioned? Is it indoors or outdoors? Are any specific places named? A field? A garden? A house?

WHEN did this take place (both in history and time of day)? Is a day of the week mentioned? Is the time of day morning, noon, evening, or night?

WHY did these people do what they did? This may or may not be directly stated. Is someone suffering? Ill? Disabled? Afraid? Obeying God? Disobeying God?

As we move forward on our adventure of discovering the wonderful truths contained in the Bible, I want you to meet another young woman from the pages of Scripture. She shows us what it means to be a woman who follows God with all her heart.

Portrait of Mary, a Young Woman After God's Own Heart

Oh, how I love this girl! As you read about the young teenage Mary, realize that she sets an example for women of all ages of what it means to follow God with all your heart. As you make your way through Luke 1:26-38, run through the set of questions and make notes in the spaces provided. This is how Bible study is done: You question each verse to observe and deal with as much information as possible. Also remember this: Not every question asked will be answered in the verse you are looking at. Some sections will remain blank.

Most of all, whatever you do, don't get discouraged. Don't give up. Just enjoy Mary's remarkable story. And, as you step into God's life-changing Word, pray the psalmist's prayer from Psalm 119:18: "Open my eyes that I may see wonderful things in your law."

> ^{26} In the sixth month of Elizabeth's pregnancy, God sent the angel Gabriel to Nazareth, a town in Galilee,

WHO are the people mentioned, and how are they described?

WHAT's happening?

WHAT places are mentioned?

WHAT references to time are recorded?

²⁷ to a virgin pledged to be married to a man named Joseph, a descendant of David. The virgin's name was Mary.

WHO are the people mentioned, and how are they described?

WHAT's happening?

WHAT places are mentioned?

WHAT references to time are recorded?

> ²⁸ The angel went to her and said, "Greetings, you who are highly favored! The Lord is with you."

WHO are the people mentioned, and how are they described?

WHAT's happening?

WHAT places are mentioned?

WHAT references to time are recorded?

[29] Mary was greatly troubled at his words and wondered what kind of greeting this might be.

WHO are the people mentioned, and how are they described?

WHAT's happening?

WHAT places are mentioned?

WHAT references to time are recorded?

[30] But the angel said to her, "Do not be afraid, Mary; you have found favor with God.

WHO are the people mentioned, and how are they described?

WHAT's happening?

WHAT places are mentioned?

WHAT references to time are recorded?

31 You will conceive and give birth to a son, and you are to call him Jesus.

WHO are the people mentioned, and how are they described?

WHAT's happening?

WHAT places are mentioned?

WHAT references to time are recorded?

> 32 He will be great and will be called the Son of
> the Most High. The Lord God will give him the
> throne of his father David,

WHO are the people mentioned, and how are they
described?

WHAT's happening?

WHAT places are mentioned?

WHAT references to time are recorded?

> ^{33} and he will reign over Jacob's descendants forever; his kingdom will never end."

WHO are the people mentioned, and how are they described?

WHAT's happening?

WHAT places are mentioned?

WHAT references to time are recorded?

34 "How will this be," Mary asked the angel, "since I am a virgin?"

WHO are the people mentioned, and how are they described?

WHAT's happening?

WHAT places are mentioned?

WHAT references to time are recorded?

35 The angel answered, "The Holy Spirit will come on you, and the power of the Most High will overshadow you. So the holy one to be born will be called the Son of God.

WHO are the people mentioned, and how are they described?

WHAT's happening?

WHAT places are mentioned?

WHAT references to time are recorded?

> 36 Even Elizabeth your relative is going to have a
> child in her old age, and she who was said to be
> unable to conceive is in her sixth month.

WHO are the people mentioned, and how are they
described?

WHAT's happening?

WHAT places are mentioned?

WHAT references to time are recorded?

37 For no word from God will ever fail.

WHO are the people mentioned, and how are they described?

WHAT's happening?

WHAT places are mentioned?

WHAT references to time are recorded?

³⁸ "I am the Lord's servant," Mary answered. "May your word to me be fulfilled." Then the angel left her.

WHO are the people mentioned, and how are they described?

WHAT's happening?

WHAT places are mentioned?

WHAT references to time are recorded?

Making It Personal

Congratulations! You have read and observed God's Word to discover the who, what, where, and when answers from Scripture. You are now ready to make it personal. This brings you to the APPLICATION step in studying the Bible. Take time to answer the questions that follow, which are designed to help you to apply God's Word to your life today—to make it personal.

Lessons on purity. In our society, a girl's purity is not always viewed as something special or even important. Sexual activity among teens is at epidemic proportions. Purity was important to God as He selected Mary to be the mother of His Son, Jesus Christ, the Messiah. God never changes, and He still sees purity as important for teen girls who want to follow Him.

How important is purity to you? What kind of commitment can you make to God to live a pure life? And what steps would help you keep your commitment?

_____

_____

_____

_____

Lessons on faith. By the age of 12 to 14 years old, Mary had already learned to trust in God and His Word. As a teen like Mary, what are you doing to cultivate your faith—to build up your trust in God?

_____

_____

_____

_____

Reflect back over this past week. How did you exhibit great faith…or not-so-great faith?

_____

_____

_____

_____

What other lessons do you want to take away from Luke 1:26-38, from Mary's encounter with the angel Gabriel?

_____

_____

_____

_____

How Do You Respond to God?

The announcement of a child's birth was met with various responses throughout Scripture. Sarah, Abraham's wife, laughed (Genesis 18:9-15). Manoah, Samson's father, panicked (Judges 13:22). Zechariah doubted (Luke 1:18). By contrast, Mary submitted. She believed the angel's words and agreed to bear the child, even under humanly impossible circumstances. God is able to do the impossible. Our response to his demands should not be laughter, fear, or doubt, but willing acceptance.[2]

Looking at Your Life

No one lives in a vacuum. You are and always will be influenced by people and your surroundings. Obviously, your parents have and will continue to provide the greatest contribution to your development. And as the years go by, there will be others. Maybe it will be a teacher, a coach, a pastor or his wife, or a best friend. I'm praying that you are surrounded with good, positive examples and influencers. But you also have to be on the alert for people who influence you negatively, who pull you down and away from what God wants for you.

How will you know if what you are experiencing from others or your surroundings is good for you? God has already provided you with a way of determining how to evaluate your life experiences. He has supplied you with the Ultimate

Guidebook to Life—the Bible. The Bible is and ought to be your greatest source of help. It will make you wise unto salvation, and it will be a lamp that will guide your steps through each day and along the treacherous road ahead.

So what do you think? Why not read the next chapter and see where it leads you? Enjoy!

9

Walking by the Spirit

I can only imagine what season of the year it is as you are reading and learning more about what your Bible says, what it means, and what you will do about it. But as I write this guide to discovering your Bible, it is spring in Washington State. And, as an added bonus, today we are enjoying a rare phenomenon in the midst of our usually rainy spring weather—the sun is shining! So like everyone else in our community, Jim and I went into town to our local hardware store. What we saw there, in addition to the throngs of happy people, was a vast array of young fruit trees ready to be purchased and planted to someday bear fruit.

As I'm thinking now about those different fruit trees, I can't help but wonder about the fruit we bear in our lives as Christian women, no matter what our age. For each of those little fruit trees in black plastic containers, someone is going to spend a lot of time planting, fertilizing, watering, pruning, spraying, and protecting them until they mature enough to produce fruit. Well, I couldn't help but ask myself—and I want to ask you too: Shouldn't we pay even more attention to our own fruitfulness and fruit-bearing—in our case, the spiritual kind of fruit?

~ BIBLE STUDY 101 ~
THE EPISTLES

In the New Testament, the epistles follow the Gospels and the book of Acts (both narrative literature). After Acts comes the next type of literature, which consists of 21 letters or *epistles* written to individuals, churches, or groups of believers. These letters address every aspect of the Christian faith and the responsibilities we have as Christians.

The Role of the Holy Spirit in Understanding the Bible

Welcome to the epistles! These letters are a different type of literature and need to be approached as if you are sitting in a classroom at school and receiving instructions from one of your teachers. That's because what you're about to learn is vitally important.

In the case of the Bible, spiritually mature teachers like the apostles Paul or Peter are your instructors. This sounds pretty heavy, right? So what if I told you that you have help—a personal private tutor—when it comes to studying and understanding your Bible? Well, you do! If you are a believer in Jesus Christ, God's Spirit is that Helper, and He plays several key roles in enabling you to understand what God says in His Word.

Read the verses that follow and describe the Holy Spirit and/or His role as you approach your study of God's Word:

However, you are not in the flesh but in the Spirit, if indeed the Spirit of God dwells in you (Romans 8:9 NASB).

_____

_____

The Advocate, the Holy Spirit, whom the Father will send in my name, will teach you all things and will remind you of everything I have said to you (John 14:26).

_____

_____

When he, the Spirit of truth, comes, he will guide you into all the truth (John 16:13).

_____

_____

Bonus question: Look again at these verses and list the different names of the Spirit of God.

_____

_____

If you stop to think about it, you will realize how important the Holy Spirit's ministry is in your life. It is the Holy Spirit who gives you the ability to understand the spiritual nature of the Bible. It is the Holy Spirit who provides the resources you need to be God's kind of young adult woman.

What is more, it is the power of the Holy Spirit within you that will exhibit itself in what is called "the fruit of the Spirit."

Before we dive into the fruit of the Spirit as listed in Galatians 5:22-23, let's learn something about this passage's CONTEXT.

~ Bible Study 101 ~
The Book of Galatians

Each letter or epistle in the New Testament was written for a purpose. It was written by someone, to someone, about something important. For example, the apostle Paul wrote the letter of Galatians to a group of people who had come to faith in Christ during his first missionary journey. False teachers followed Paul into the same region and told the people they needed to keep the law of Moses in addition to accepting and believing in Christ. Paul wrote this letter to remind the people that faith in Jesus was all they needed, that Jesus had set them free from the law. Chapters 1–4 of Galatians present an explanation of the principles or the doctrines of the Christian faith. Chapters 5–6 is the practical section of Galatians and reveals the power of faith as exhibited in a Christian's daily spiritual walk.

With this information about the CONTEXT of the book of Galatians in mind, read Galatians 5:22-23 below and circle each character quality that is part of the fruit that is produced by the Holy Spirit. Then go one step further and underline the character quality you think you need the most help with.

> The fruit of the Spirit is love, joy, peace, patience, kindness, goodness, faithfulness, gentleness, self-control (NASB).

The Fruit of the Spirit

In the Bible, "fruit" refers to the external evidence of what is within. Any person who has received Jesus as Savior has the Lord living within them, and that indwelling of God's Holy Spirit will evidence itself as good "fruit," or godly character. Using the step of CROSS-REFERENCING will help you discover the meaning of each aspect of the fruit of the Spirit and what your life looks like when you exhibit God's fruit. Here we go!

You will exhibit love.

According to the Bible, love is self-sacrifice. We tend to think of love as an emotion, but it's really an act of the will. It's a deliberate decision to choose to care about and help others. Read the following verses and describe how God the Father and His Son, Jesus, demonstrated this principle:

> God so loved the world that he gave his one and only Son (John 3:16).

_____

_____

_____

> The Son of Man [Jesus] did not come to be served,
> but to serve, and to give his life (Matthew 20:28).

_____

_____

_____

Jesus "resolutely set out for Jerusalem" (Luke 9:51), where He would die on the cross for us.

_____

_____

Summary: Giving, serving, heading for Jerusalem, and dying on a cross. Jesus did all of this and more for His own, including you. These are definitely not emotional responses. They are deliberate acts of the will born out of love.

Personal application: It's easy to be the smiling life of the party with your friends, to do anything and everything for them. However, your main arena for love is at home with the members of your family—even your pesky, irritating brothers and sisters! So how can you be more giving and more helpful at home? Moms and dads can always use help, and so can brothers and sisters. What can—and will—you begin to do on a daily basis to give and serve at home to love your family?

List at least one action you will take right away.

_____

_____

_____

> Love involves effort, not merely emotion.
> Love demands action, not just feelings.
> Love is something you do,
> not something you only feel or say.[1]

You will exhibit joy.

When the sun is shining brightly in your life and there are no problems, it's easy to be happy. But when life turns black and stormy and things aren't going so well, you are not quite so happy, right? This is where people confuse the human emotion of happiness with true spiritual joy. A good definition for you to remember is that joy is "the sacrifice of praise." So even when things aren't going well or your heart hurts, there are some actions you can take to find and exhibit joy. What do these scriptures advise you to do when you encounter trials and problems?

> Give thanks in all circumstances; for this is God's will for you in Christ Jesus (1 Thessalonians 5:18).

_____

_____

_____

> Consider it pure joy, my brothers and sisters, whenever you face trials of many kinds (James 1:2).

_____

_____

_____

> Rejoice in the Lord always. I will say it again: Rejoice! (Philippians 4:4).

"Rejoice in _____."

OBSERVATION: What reference is made to time?

_____

Personal application: "In the Lord" is where your joy begins, exists, and is generated toward others. Joy has nothing to do with your situation, but everything to do with your relationship with Jesus. When Jesus' Spirit is controlling your life, you can experience joy anywhere, anytime, no matter what's happening!

Name the greatest trial or disappointment you are currently facing. Then willfully lift your situation up to the Lord and rejoice. This will help you get your mind off your problem and onto God!

_____

_____

> Joy is not dependent on circumstances,
> but on the spiritual realities of God's goodness.
> Joy is not merely an emotion,
> but the result of choosing to look beyond
> what appears to be true in your life to
> what is true about your life in Christ.[2]

You will experience peace.

My slogan for peace is "the sacrifice of trust." You and I make the sacrifice of trust when we face pain and stress in our lives and choose to trust God instead of stressing out. In the verses that follow, identify the reasons you can fully trust God and experience His peace.

> Since we have been justified through faith, we have peace with God through our Lord Jesus Christ (Romans 5:1).

_____

_____

> Do not be anxious about anything, but in every situation, by prayer and petition, with thanksgiving, present your requests to God. And the peace of God, which transcends all understanding, will guard your hearts and your minds in Christ Jesus (Philippians 4:6-7).

_____

_____

_____

Personal application: Being angry, frazzled, freaked out, or a nervous wreck can become a life habit. But remembering to look to God and trust that He is in full control of your life gives you the peace you need to handle life's speed bumps, roadblocks, and detours. Which of these two verses will you remember this week when you feel like you are falling apart and can't possibly handle your responsibilities or relationships?

_____

_____

> Peace comes with knowing that
> your heavenly Father is continually with you.
> Peace also comes with acknowledging that
> God will supply your every need.[3]

You will exhibit patience.

Patience is choosing to wait and do nothing. This may be waiting for a few seconds before you say or do something mean, and instead, backing away and cooling off until you can determine the best way to respond—or to not respond at all! Patience has the ability to wait and wait for a long time, if necessary. CONSULTATION: Write out the dictionary meaning for *patience*:

_____

_____

_____

Using this same dictionary, list several antonyms (words that give the opposite meaning) for *patience*.

_____

_____

_____

After you list the antonyms, circle the ones that describe how you normally respond in your daily activities. What does this indicate about your "walk" with God, and what will you do to remind yourself to look to God for His patience in all situations?

_____

_____

_____

> Patience is a key to harmony in relationships.
> It is a practical first step to getting along with people.[4]

You will exhibit kindness.

While your patience waits and does nothing sinful (like getting mad or yelling in anger), kindness now plans for godly action. What are the three commands in this verse?

> Be kind and compassionate to one another, forgiving each other, just as in Christ God forgave you (Ephesians 4:32).

_____

_____

_____

> The highest compliment a Christian woman
> can receive is to be described as "too nice."[5]
>
> Kindness is the ability to love people more
> than they deserve.[6]

You will exhibit goodness.

Here's a handle for understanding goodness—goodness
does everything! In other words, goodness does everything
it can to shower God's goodness upon others. What do these
verses say about goodness?

> Love your enemies, do good to those who hate
> you (Luke 6:27).

_____

_____

Everyone has "enemies." What will you do the next time
you are up against one of your enemies? What will you say?
How will you act—or not act? Plan ahead and be prepared
to respond in goodness.

_____

_____

_____

We are God's handiwork, created in Christ Jesus to do good works, which God prepared in advance for us to do (Ephesians 2:10).

> Do all the good you can,
> by all the means you can,
> in all the ways you can,
> in all the places you can,
> at all the times you can,
> to all the people you can,
> as long as ever you can.[7]

You will exhibit faithfulness.

Faithfulness is a mind-set that says "Just do it!" Faithfulness is choosing to do what you should do, no matter what. When you make a decision to do something, you don't make excuses. You look to God for His strength and purpose to keep your word. Even with the tough decisions, God will give you everything you need to fulfill your responsibilities. Faithfulness does not allow tiredness, laziness, or any other challenge to divert completing any promised task that comes your way.

> Women must likewise be dignified, not malicious gossips, but temperate, faithful in all things (1 Timothy 3:11 NASB).

In the verse above, circle the four qualities required in the women who serve in their church. What does the verse say about faithfulness?

_____

The Hero
The hero does not set out to be one.
Being where he was supposed to be...
doing what he was supposed to do...
responding as was his custom...
to circumstances as they developed...
devoted to duty—he did the heroic.[8]

You will exhibit gentleness.

Gentleness does not mean weakness, but actually has the idea of meekness—"strength under control." A young woman who is characterized by gentleness is willing to endure unkind behavior and suffering. Instead of giving in to emotions, she places her full trust in God's wisdom, power, and love. In the eyes of the world, gentleness may look like weakness, but it actually shows the greatest kind of strength!

> Blessed are the gentle [humble, meek], for they shall inherit the earth (Matthew 5:5 NASB).

What did Jesus say about those who are gentle?

_____

_____

Your beauty should not come from outward
adornment...Rather, it should be that of your
inner self, the unfading beauty of a gentle and
quiet spirit (1 Peter 3:3-4).

What did Peter say about a woman's beauty?

It should not be _____

_____

_____

It should be _____

_____

_____

A Prayer for Gentleness

Thou who art meek and lowly of heart,
teach me to be meek, give me a meekness
that shall pass through every ordeal. Amen.[9]

You will exhibit self-control.

Self-control chooses not to think or do what you know
is against God's Word. You choose not to excuse or baby or
indulge yourself. You refuse to take the easy way out. You
don't rationalize your wrong cravings in an attempt to make
them legitimate, and you certainly don't just follow the crowd.

Rather, you resolve to say, "No!"—no to wrong thoughts, wrong attitudes, and wrong behaviors.

Look up 1 Corinthians 10:31 in your Bible. Write it out below and circle what this verse says about why you should desire self-control. Then memorize the verse—and be sure you do it!

_____

_____

_____

_____

> The word *self-control* means "the ability to say no."
> It is an evidence of willpower that sometimes
> expresses itself in "won't power."[10]

The Art of Walking

Okay! You now have a basic understanding of the fruit of the Spirit. So let's move on to some APPLICATION. How can you put this new understanding to work in your life?

The "fruit of the Spirit" that you have just inspected is an expression of God's nature that indwells believers. The fruit of the Spirit is God's spiritual power in you on parade for all to see. When you walk by the Spirit, you exhibit godly behavior—the fruit of the Spirit.

So I say, walk by the Spirit, and you will not gratify the desires of the flesh (Galatians 5:16).

What happens when you are walking by the Spirit?

_____

_____

In simple terms, walking in or by the Spirit means *living each moment in submission to God*. It means *wanting to do the right thing and letting God guide you each step of the way.* Unfortunately, as you already know, walking in the Sprit isn't easy, and that's an understatement! But Jesus gives us the solution to our struggle. Write it out below.

> I am the vine, you are the branches; he who abides ["remains"—NIV] in Me and I in him, he bears much fruit, for apart from Me you can do nothing (John 15:5 NASB).

_____

_____

When you abide, remain, or stay near Jesus, you will bear the spiritual fruit of love, joy, peace, patience, kindness, goodness, faithfulness, gentleness, and self-control. Now for one final question: What did Jesus say is involved in remaining close to Him?

> If you keep My commandments, you will abide ["remain"—NIV] in My love (John 15:10 NASB).

_____

_____

Looking at Your Life

Isn't the Bible an amazing book? God Himself communicates to you on the pages in your Bible. So how about some APPLICATION? This is the step in Bible study that requires you to ask and answer the question, "What am I going to do about what I'm learning?"

God wants you, as His child, to know Him better and better every single day. To do this you need to grow spiritually—to grow as a believer in Christ, to grow as a daughter, a sister, and a friend. And here's the key: If you obey His commands and walk by His Spirit, you will experience spiritual growth and the power of the Holy Spirit. You will exhibit the fruit of the Spirit.

10

Becoming More Like Jesus

Can you believe you are at the end—or at least the final chapter—of your journey into understanding your Bible? If we were face-to-face, believe me, I'd be hugging you and giving you an enthusiastic high five, and you and I would be seriously planning a celebration, maybe a trip for pizza and ice cream.

By now you have picked up on why studying your Bible is important. Your Bible is not just any old, antiquated book from the past. As you've looked into it for yourself and made multiple life-changing applications to your life, it's become so much more than white pages and black ink with a whole lot of words!

No, the Bible takes great care to let you know that it is the Word of God. It claims to have been authored by God Himself and contains a message of utmost importance—a message that offers life, not just for the present, but for all eternity. This makes the Bible special, unique, one-of-a-kind, and something definitely worthy of your time, attention, and study. As you understand God's message, you gain an understanding of God Himself.

And what is God's message? The whole Bible is built around the beautiful story of Jesus Christ and His promise of eternal life for those who accept Him as God and Savior. The main reason for interpreting what the Bible says is that you might understand, know, believe, and then wholeheartedly follow Jesus. This message was so important that God took the initiative to speak—to "reveal" Himself—to mankind in the New Testament in the form of His Son, the Lord Jesus Christ, "whom he appointed heir of all things, and through whom also he made the universe" (Hebrews 1:2).

Things are about to get a little heavy as we head into the subject of prophecy, which teaches us that Jesus is coming again. So take a minute to read several brief "Bible Study 101" explanations...and then sit back and enjoy Jesus. He is the message of the Bible!

~ BIBLE STUDY 101 ~

REVELATION

The word *revelation* means "to uncover or to reveal." From the very first verse of the Bible in Genesis, God speaks, revealing Himself to mankind. Beginning with His first act of creation, He unfolds the details of His eternal plan for people. With each successive book of the Bible, we witness Him guiding the human race toward His ultimate purpose of redeeming His lost creation through His Son, Jesus Christ.

~ BIBLE STUDY 101 ~
PROPHECY

The type of Bible literature known as prophecy deals with future events. The books of Isaiah through Malachi in the Old Testament and the New Testament book of Revelation are prophecy. When it comes to the prophecies of Jesus the Messiah, many of the books of the Old Testament predict and describe His birth, life, and even His death. The Old Testament set the stage with its prophecies of the first coming of the Messiah, and the New Testament describes how Christ's first coming was accomplished and fulfilled. And in both the Old and New Testaments, we find passages that talk about Christ's second coming, or His future return to earth.

~ BIBLE STUDY 101 ~
APOCALYPTIC LITERATURE

The word *apocalypse* means "to uncover." The book of Daniel (in the Old Testament) and the book of Revelation (in the New Testament) are called apocalyptic literature. They describe cataclysmic events in which God completes what He began when mankind fell into sin in the Garden of Eden by judging sin, Satan, and his followers, and creating a new heaven and earth that is free from all sin.

Old Testament Prophecies

Isaiah was one of the greatest Old Testament prophets. Seven hundred years before the birth of Jesus, Isaiah gave an unbelievable prophecy. Underline each description of the child that was to come.

> For to us a child is born, to us a son is given, and the government will be on his shoulders. And he will be called Wonderful Counselor, Mighty God, Everlasting Father, Prince of Peace. Of the greatness of his government and peace there will be no end. He will reign on David's throne and over his kingdom, establishing and upholding it with justice and righteousness from that time on and forever (Isaiah 9:6-7).

In the New Testament, we see the fulfillment of this prophecy. How does this New Testament verse describe the fulfillment of Isaiah's prediction?

> God so loved the world that he gave his one and only Son, that whoever believes in him shall not perish but have eternal life (John 3:16).

_____

_____

_____

What was the prophet Micah's prediction in 700 BC?

> But you, Bethlehem Ephrathah, though you are small among the clans of Judah, out of you will

come for me one who will be ruler over Israel,
whose origins are from of old, from ancient
times (Micah 5:2).

_____

_____

_____

What does the New Testament say happened in a little town
called Bethlehem—700 years after Micah's prediction?

Joseph also went up from the town of Nazareth
in Galilee to Judea, to Bethlehem the town of
David, because he belonged to the house and
line of David. He went there to register with
Mary, who was pledged to be married to him
and was expecting a child. While they were
there, the time came for the baby to be born...
(Luke 2:4-6).

_____

_____

_____

Personal application: Do you have trust issues when it
comes to the Bible and believing what it says? Evaluate your
level of trust. How do just these two fulfilled prophecies
encourage your faith in the Word of God?

_____

_____

Why Did Jesus Come into the World?

In chapter 1 we got a good look at Eve in Genesis 3. I'm sure you remember what happened to Eve. She disobeyed God's one and only rule...and ate the forbidden fruit. That act of disobedience ushered sin into the perfect world God created.

How are we to view sin? The world defines sin as no big deal—it's nothing you need to worry about. Nothing that has any earth-shattering consequences. Hey, if it feels good, it must be okay.

But sin is much more serious than that! Sin as defined in the Bible is anything that is contrary to God's holy standards in thought, word, or deed. And because God is holy, He must judge sin, just as He judged Eve and Adam's sin of disobedience. So as you can see, anyone who sins has a very big problem—including you and me.

How did Jesus summarize God's standard?

Be perfect, therefore, as your heavenly Father is perfect (Matthew 5:48).

According to the verse below, how many people meet God's standard of perfection?

> There is no one who does good, not even one (Romans 3:12).

_____

_____

That brings us to a very important question: Why did Jesus come into the world? What answer does the Bible give?

> The Son of Man came to seek and to save the lost (Luke 19:10).

_____

_____

> Christ Jesus came into the world to save sinners (1 Timothy 1:15).

_____

_____

Why Did Jesus Have to Die?

God is Spirit and cannot die. Christ, being God, took on a body of flesh and blood to make it possible for Him to die in order to pay the price for our sins.

According to the verses that follow, what did Jesus' death accomplish?

> I have come that they may have life, and have it to the full (John 10:10).

_____

_____

> Christ also suffered once for sins, the righteous for the unrighteous, to bring you to God (1 Peter 3:18).

_____

_____

> God made [Jesus] who had no sin to be sin for us, so that in [Jesus] we might become the righteousness of God (2 Corinthians 5:21).

_____

_____

> [Christ] gave himself for our sins to rescue us from the present evil age (Galatians 1:4).

_____

_____

Such sacrifice demands a personal response. In the scriptures below, what should be your response toward Jesus?

> To all who did receive him, to those who believed in his name, he gave the right to become children of God (John 1:12).

Response: _____

Result: _____

> God presented Christ as a sacrifice of atonement, through the shedding of his blood—to be received by faith (Romans 3:25).

Response: _____

What are some results that follow a decision to receive Christ as Savior?

> God, who is rich in mercy, made us alive with Christ even when we were dead in transgressions (Ephesians 2:4-5).

_____

_____

> Since we have been justified through faith, we have peace with God through our Lord Jesus Christ (Romans 5:1).

_____

_____

Heart to heart: My friend, have you personally received Christ as your Savior and received His payment for your sin? If you have, pause and remember the details of that life-changing decision, and thank God with all your heart. If you haven't or you aren't sure, take a moment now to pray. Tell God you want to know the truth, and you want to respond to it—that you want to know Jesus. Reach out and ask questions of those who can give you answers. Call out to Jesus as one man did in Mark 9:24: "Help me overcome my unbelief!"

~ BIBLE STUDY 101 ~
ESCHATOLOGY

The Bible has proven itself reliable in the fulfillment of its predictions. God's prophets said the Messiah would come—and He did. But God isn't finished. There is more to come. Regardless of how dark and desperate the world is today, God continues to move toward His victorious plan. Bible scholars call this movement toward the future *eschatology*, or the study of last things.

Jesus Is Coming Again!

Yes, it's true! The Bible says Jesus is coming again. As you read the thrilling scriptures below, write out the truths and promises they contain about Jesus' return.

> "Men of Galilee," they said, "why do you stand here looking into the sky? This same Jesus, who has been taken from you into heaven, will come back in the same way you have seen him go into heaven" (Acts 1:11).

_____

_____

My Father's house has many rooms; if that were not so, would I have told you that I am going there to prepare a place for you? (John 14:2).

_____

_____

If I go and prepare a place for you, I will come back and take you to be with me that you also may be where I am (John 14:3).

_____

_____

There are some people who say that if Jesus has not returned yet, then He will never return. They don't believe He will come back. However, what does the apostle Peter say is the reason for Christ's delay in coming again?

The Lord is not slow in keeping his promise, as some understand slowness. Instead he is patient with you, not wanting anyone to perish, but everyone to come to repentance (2 Peter 3:9).

_____

_____

_____

Personal application: The Bible is accurate in its predictions about both Jesus' first coming and His return. What does the verse below say you should be doing to prepare for His return?

> Since everything will be destroyed...what kind of people ought you to be? You ought to live holy and godly lives (2 Peter 3:11).

_____

_____

How can you live a holy and godly life as you wait for Jesus' return? The answer is, by becoming more like Jesus.

Becoming More Like Jesus

In my book *A Young Woman Who Reflects the Heart of Jesus*,[1] I highlighted 12 character qualities Jesus possessed that you and I can—and should—reflect. One way to grow more like Jesus is to *want* to emulate Him in as many ways as possible. By looking at Jesus day in and day out, and studying His life, you will be changed—transformed into His image—as you follow in His steps. Here are three qualities to get you started in becoming more like Jesus.

Be a servant—Look at Matthew 20:28. The purpose of Jesus' life was to give—to give everything, even His very life.

> The Son of Man did not come to be served, but to serve, and to give his life as a ransom for many (Matthew 20:28).

Personal application: What can you do today—and every day—to be more like Jesus and be a servant at home and in public?

_____

_____

_____

Be a woman of prayer—When you get a little extra time, take a look in your Bible at Jesus praying before He made important decisions (Luke 6:12-13) and praying as He prepared to go to the cross (Matthew 26:39-46). A good principle for your life—and your decision making—is "No decision made without prayer." Even in a split second you can address God and pray, "Lord, what is the right thing to do?" At every minute and in every situation, how does turning to God in prayer help you, as seen in the verse below?

> Let us then approach God's throne of grace with confidence, so that we may receive mercy and find grace to help us in our time of need (Hebrews 4:16).

_____

_____

_____

Be pure—Purity doesn't just happen. It doesn't come naturally. In fact, the opposite is what comes naturally! So you must make an effort to avoid people, places, and practices that tempt you in the wrong direction—that tempt you to disobey God's standards of purity. Jot down the three steps this verse gives you for staying pure:

> Flee the evil desires of youth and pursue righteousness, faith, love and peace, along with those who call on the Lord out of a pure heart (2 Timothy 2:22).

Run away from _____

_____

Pursue _____

_____

Associate with _____

_____

I'm praying you will grasp how very special Jesus is as your Lord and Savior, and see Him as the perfect model for how to live your life.

In praying, you will

— grasp _____ ,

— see Him as _____ , and

— set your heart on becoming more like Jesus.

Looking at Your Life

My dear reading friend, we have come to the end of this brief, bare-bones introduction to Bible study. You've hung in there to the end. You've wrestled with lots of technical information. And you've done the work. I wish I could give you a "Certificate of Completion"—accept my hearty congratulations!

As we both prepare to go our separate ways, there is one really important thing I want you to remember about studying the Bible. The ultimate goal of Bible study is not to do something to the Bible. It's not to merely circle or underline words, or fill in blanks, or make sure you know what happened before or after a particular verse. No, the ultimate goal of Bible study is to have the Bible do something to you!

The primary purpose of Bible study is not to increase your knowledge, but to change your heart and your life! That is why, from page 1 of this book, I knew I wanted to end our study looking at Jesus, drawing closer to Jesus, reveling in Jesus, and worshipping Jesus. The whole purpose of learning how to study the Bible is so that all believers—including you—will be conformed to the image of Jesus.

And now, my precious new friend, "to him who is able to keep you from stumbling and to present you before his glorious presence without fault and with great joy—to the only God our Savior be glory, and majesty, power and authority, through Jesus Christ our Lord, before all ages, now and forevermore! Amen."

Appendix 1

How to Study the Bible—
Some Practical Tips

One of the noblest pursuits a child of God can embark upon is to get to know and understand God better. The best way we can accomplish this is to look carefully at the book He has written, the Bible, which communicates who He is and His plan for mankind. There are a number of ways we can study the Bible, but one of the most effective and simple approaches to reading and understanding God's Word involves three simple steps:

Step 1: Observation—*What does the passage say?*
Step 2: Interpretation—*What does the passage
        mean?*
Step 3: Application—*What am I going to do about
        what the passage says and means?*

Observation is the first and most important step in the process. As you read the Bible text, you need to look carefully at what is said, and how it is said. Look for:

❈ *Terms, not words.* Words can have many meanings, but terms are words used in a specific way in a specific context. (For instance, the word *trunk* could apply to a tree, a car, or a storage box. However, when you read, "That tree has a very large trunk," you know exactly what the word means, which makes it a term.)

❈ *Structure.* If you look at your Bible, you will see that the text has units called paragraphs (indented or marked ¶). A paragraph is a complete unit of thought. You can discover the content of the author's message by noting and understanding each paragraph unit.

❈ *Emphasis.* The amount of space or the number of chapters or verses devoted to a specific topic will reveal the importance of that topic (for example, note the emphasis of Romans 9–11 and Psalm 119).

❈ *Repetition.* This is another way an author demonstrates that something is important. One reading of 1 Corinthians 13, where the author uses the word "love" nine times in only 13 verses, communicates to us that love is the focal point of these 13 verses.

❈ *Relationships between ideas.* Pay close attention, for example, to certain relationships that appear in the text:

— Cause and effect: "Well done, good and faithful servant; you were faithful over a few things, I will make you ruler over many things" (Matthew 25:21 NKJV).

— Ifs and thens: "If My people who are called by My name will humble themselves, and pray and seek My face, and turn from their wicked ways, then I will hear from heaven, and will forgive their sin and heal their land" (2 Chronicles 7:14 NKJV).

— Questions and answers: "Who is this King of glory? The LORD strong and mighty" (Psalm 24:8).

❋ *Comparisons and contrasts.* For example, "You have heard that it was said...But I say to you..." (Matthew 5:21-22 NKJV).

❋ *Literary form.* The Bible is literature, and the three main types of literature in the Bible are discourse (the epistles), prose (Old Testament history), and poetry (the Psalms). Considering the type of literature makes a great deal of difference when you read and interpret the Scriptures.

❋ *Atmosphere.* The author had a particular reason or burden for writing each passage, chapter, and book. Be sure you notice the mood or tone or urgency of the writing.

After you have considered these things, you then are ready to ask the WH questions:

Who?	Who are the people in this passage?
What?	What is happening in this passage?
Where?	Where is this story taking place?
When?	What time (of day, of the year, in history) is it?

Asking these four WH questions can help you notice terms and identify atmosphere. The answers will also enable you to use your imagination to recreate the scene you're reading about.

As you answer the WH questions and imagine the event, you'll probably come up with some questions of your own. Asking those additional questions for understanding will help to build a bridge between observation (the first step) and interpretation (the second step) of the Bible study process.

Interpretation is discovering the meaning of a passage, the author's main thought or idea. Answering the questions that arise during observation will help you in the process of interpretation. Five clues (called "the five C's") can help you determine the author's main point(s):

❀ *Context*. You can answer 75 percent of your questions about a passage when you read the text. Reading the text involves looking at the near context (the verse immediately before and after) as well as the far context (the paragraph or the chapter that precedes and/or follows the passage you're studying).

❀ *Cross-references*. Let Scripture interpret Scripture. That is, let other passages in the Bible shed light on the passage you are looking at. At the same time, be careful not to assume that the same word or phrase in two different passages means the same thing.

❀ *Culture*. The Bible was written long ago, so when we interpret it, we need to understand it from the writers' cultural context.

❊ *Conclusion*. Having answered your questions for understanding by means of context, cross-reference, and culture, you can make a preliminary statement of the passage's meaning. Remember that if your passage consists of more than one paragraph, the author may be presenting more than one thought or idea.

❊ *Consultation*. Reading books known as commentaries, which are written by Bible scholars, can help you interpret Scripture.

Application is why we study the Bible. We want our lives to change; we want to be obedient to God and to grow more like Jesus Christ. After we have observed a passage and interpreted or understood it to the best of our ability, we must then apply its truth to our own life.

You'll want to ask the following questions of every passage of Scripture you study:

❊ How does the truth revealed here affect my relationship with God?

❊ How does this truth affect my relationship with others?

❊ How does this truth affect me?

❊ How does this truth affect my response to the enemy, Satan?

The application step is not completed by simply answering these questions; the key is *putting into practice* what God has taught you in your study. Although at any given moment you cannot be consciously applying *every*thing you're learning in

Bible study, you can be consciously applying *something*. And when you work on applying a truth to your life, God will bless your efforts by, as noted earlier, conforming you to the image of Jesus Christ.

Helpful Bible Study Resources:

Concordance—Young's or Strong's
Bible dictionary—Unger's or Holman's
Webster's dictionary
The Zondervan Pictorial Encyclopedia of the Bible
Manners and Customs of the Bible,
James M. Freeman

Books on Bible Study:

The Joy of Discovery, Oletta Wald
Enjoy Your Bible, Irving L. Jensen
How to Read the Bible for All It's Worth, Gordon
Fee & Douglas Stuart
A Layman's Guide to Interpreting the Bible,
W. Henrichsen
Living by the Book, Howard G. Hendricks

Appendix 2

A One-Year Daily Bible Reading Plan

January

Genesis
- ☐ 1   1–3
- ☐ 2   4–7
- ☐ 3   8–11
- ☐ 4   12–15
- ☐ 5   16–18
- ☐ 6   19–22
- ☐ 7   23–27
- ☐ 8   28–30
- ☐ 9   31–34
- ☐ 10 35–38
- ☐ 11 39–41
- ☐ 12 42–44
- ☐ 13 45–47
- ☐ 14 48–50

Exodus
- ☐ 15 1–4
- ☐ 16 5–7
- ☐ 17 8–11
- ☐ 18 12–14
- ☐ 19 15–18
- ☐ 20 19–21
- ☐ 21 22–24
- ☐ 22 25–28
- ☐ 23 29–31
- ☐ 24 32–34
- ☐ 25 35–37
- ☐ 26 38–40

Leviticus
- ☐ 27 1–3
- ☐ 28 4–6
- ☐ 29 7–9
- ☐ 30 10–13
- ☐ 31 14–16

February

- ☐ 1   17–20
- ☐ 2   21–23
- ☐ 3   24–27

Numbers
- ☐ 4   1–2
- ☐ 5   3–4

❑ 6	5–6		❑ 8	15–17
❑ 7	7–8		❑ 9	18–21
❑ 8	9–10		❑ 10	22–24
❑ 9	11–13			
❑ 10	14–15		**Judges**	
❑ 11	16–17		❑ 11	1–3
❑ 12	18–19		❑ 12	4–6
❑ 13	20–21		❑ 13	7–9
❑ 14	22–23		❑ 14	10–12
❑ 15	24–26		❑ 15	13–15
❑ 16	27–29		❑ 16	16–18
❑ 17	30–32		❑ 17	19–21
❑ 18	33–36			

Deuteronomy

Ruth

❑ 18   1–4

❑ 19	1–2		**1 Samuel**	
❑ 20	3–4		❑ 19	1–3
❑ 21	5–7		❑ 20	4–6
❑ 22	8–10		❑ 21	7–9
❑ 23	11–13		❑ 22	10–12
❑ 24	14–16		❑ 23	13–14
❑ 25	17–20		❑ 24	15–16
❑ 26	21–23		❑ 25	17–18
❑ 27	24–26		❑ 26	19–20
❑ 28	27–28		❑ 27	21–23
			❑ 28	24–26
			❑ 29	27–29
			❑ 30	30–31

March

❑ 1	29–30		**2 Samuel**	
❑ 2	31–32		❑ 31	1–3
❑ 3	33–34			

Joshua

April

❑ 4	1–4		❑ 1	4–6
❑ 5	5–7		❑ 2	7–10
❑ 6	8–10			
❑ 7	11–14			

❏ 3   11–13
❏ 4   14–15
❏ 5   16–17
❏ 6   18–20
❏ 7   21–22
❏ 8   23–24

1 Kings
❏ 9   1–2
❏ 10   3–5
❏ 11   6–7
❏ 12   8–9
❏ 13   10–12
❏ 14   13–15
❏ 15   16–18
❏ 16   19–20
❏ 17   21–22

2 Kings
❏ 18   1–3
❏ 19   4–6
❏ 20   7–8
❏ 21   9–11
❏ 22   12–14
❏ 23   15–17
❏ 24   18–19
❏ 25   20–22
❏ 26   23–25

1 Chronicles
❏ 27   1–2
❏ 28   3–5
❏ 29   6–7
❏ 30   8–10

May
❏ 1   11–13
❏ 2   14–16
❏ 3   17–19
❏ 4   20–22
❏ 5   23–25
❏ 6   26–27
❏ 7   28–29

2 Chronicles
❏ 8   1–4
❏ 9   5–7
❏ 10   8–10
❏ 11   11–14
❏ 12   15–18
❏ 13   19–21
❏ 14   22–25
❏ 15   26–28
❏ 16   29–31
❏ 17   32–33
❏ 18   34–36

Ezra
❏ 19   1–4
❏ 20   5–7
❏ 21   8–10

Nehemiah
❏ 22   1–3
❏ 23   4–7

❏ 24   8–10
❏ 25   11–13

Esther
❏ 26   1–3
❏ 27   4–7
❏ 28   8–10

Job
❏ 29   1–4
❏ 30   5–8
❏ 31   9–12

June

❏ 1   13–16
❏ 2   17–20
❏ 3   21–24
❏ 4   25–30
❏ 5   31–34
❏ 6   35–38
❏ 7   39–42

Psalms
❏ 8   1–8
❏ 9   9–17
❏ 10   18–21
❏ 11   22–28
❏ 12   29–34
❏ 13   35–39
❏ 14   40–44
❏ 15   45–50
❏ 16   51–56
❏ 17   57–63
❏ 18   64–69
❏ 19   70–74
❏ 20   75–78

❏ 21   79–85
❏ 22   86–90
❏ 23   91–98
❏ 24   99–104
❏ 25   105–107
❏ 26   108–113
❏ 27   114–118
❏ 28   119
❏ 29   120–134
❏ 30   135–142

July

❏ 1   143–150

Proverbs
❏ 2   1–3
❏ 3   4–7
❏ 4   8–11
❏ 5   12–15
❏ 6   16–18
❏ 7   19–21
❏ 8   22–24
❏ 9   25–28
❏ 10   29–31

Ecclesiastes
❏ 11   1–4
❏ 12   5–8
❏ 13   9–12

Song of Songs
❏ 14   1–4
❏ 15   5–8

Isaiah
❏ 16   1–4

❑ 17	5–8
❑ 18	9–12
❑ 19	13–15
❑ 20	16–20
❑ 21	21–24
❑ 22	25–28
❑ 23	29–32
❑ 24	33–36
❑ 25	37–40
❑ 26	41–43
❑ 27	44–46
❑ 28	47–49
❑ 29	50–52
❑ 30	53–56
❑ 31	57–60

August

❑ 1	61–63
❑ 2	64–66

Jeremiah

❑ 3	1–3
❑ 4	4–6
❑ 5	7–9
❑ 6	10–12
❑ 7	13–15
❑ 8	16–19
❑ 9	20–22
❑ 10	23–25
❑ 11	26–29
❑ 12	30–31
❑ 13	32–34
❑ 14	35–37
❑ 15	38–40
❑ 16	41–44
❑ 17	45–48

❑ 18	49–50
❑ 19	51–52

Lamentations

❑ 20	1–2
❑ 21	3–5

Ezekiel

❑ 22	1–4
❑ 23	5–8
❑ 24	9–12
❑ 25	13–15
❑ 26	16–17
❑ 27	18–20
❑ 28	21–23
❑ 29	24–26
❑ 30	27–29
❑ 31	30–31

September

❑ 1	32–33
❑ 2	34–36
❑ 3	37–39
❑ 4	40–42
❑ 5	43–45
❑ 6	46–48

Daniel

❑ 7	1–2
❑ 8	3–4
❑ 9	5–6
❑ 10	7–9
❑ 11	10–12

Hosea

❑ 12	1–4

❏ 13   5–9
❏ 14   10–14

❏ 15   **Joel**

Amos
❏ 16   1–4
❏ 17   5–9

❏ 18   **Obadiah** and **Jonah**

Micah
❏ 19   1–4
❏ 20   5–7

❏ 21   **Nahum**

❏ 22   **Habakkuk**

❏ 23   **Zephaniah**

❏ 24   **Haggai**

Zechariah
❏ 25   1–4
❏ 26   5–9
❏ 27   10–14

❏ 28   **Malachi**

Matthew
❏ 29   1–4
❏ 30   5–7

October

❏ 1   8–9
❏ 2   10–11
❏ 3   12–13
❏ 4   14–16
❏ 5   17–18
❏ 6   19–20
❏ 7   21–22
❏ 8   23–24
❏ 9   25–26
❏ 10   27–28

Mark
❏ 11   1–3
❏ 12   4–5
❏ 13   6–7
❏ 14   8–9
❏ 15   10–11
❏ 16   12–13
❏ 17   14
❏ 18   15–16

Luke
❏ 19   1–2
❏ 20   3–4
❏ 21   5–6
❏ 22   7–8
❏ 23   9–10
❏ 24   11–12
❏ 25   13–14
❏ 26   15–16
❏ 27   17–18
❏ 28   19–20
❏ 29   21–22
❏ 30   23–24

John

❏ 31   1–3

November

❏ 1   4–5
❏ 2   6–7
❏ 3   8–9
❏ 4   10–11
❏ 5   12–13
❏ 6   14–16
❏ 7   17–19
❏ 8   20–21

Acts

❏ 9   1–3
❏ 10   4–5
❏ 11   6–7
❏ 12   8–9
❏ 13   10–11
❏ 14   12–13
❏ 15   14–15
❏ 16   16–17
❏ 17   18–19
❏ 18   20–21
❏ 19   22–23
❏ 20   24–26
❏ 21   27–28

Romans

❏ 22   1–3
❏ 23   4–6
❏ 24   7–9
❏ 25   10–12
❏ 26   13–14
❏ 27   15–16

1 Corinthians

❏ 28   1–4
❏ 29   5–7
❏ 30   8–10

December

❏ 1   11–13
❏ 2   14–16

2 Corinthians

❏ 3   1–4
❏ 4   5–9
❏ 5   10–13

Galatians

❏ 6   1–3
❏ 7   4–6

Ephesians

❏ 8   1–3
❏ 9   4–6

❏ 10   **Philippians**

❏ 11   **Colossians**

❏ 12   **1 Thessalonians**

❏ 13   **2 Thessalonians**

❏ 14   **1 Timothy**

❏ 15   **2 Timothy**

❏ 16   **Titus** and **Philemon**

Hebrews
- ❑ 17   1–4
- ❑ 18   5–8
- ❑ 19   9–10
- ❑ 20   11–13

- ❑ 21   **James**

- ❑ 22   **1 Peter**

- ❑ 23   **2 Peter**

- ❑ 24   **1 John**

- ❑ 25   **2, 3 John, Jude**

Revelation
- ❑ 26   1–3
- ❑ 27   4–8
- ❑ 28   9–12
- ❑ 29   13–16
- ❑ 30   17–19
- ❑ 31   20–22

Quiet Times Calendar

Jan.	Feb.	Mar.	Apr.	May	June
1	1	1	1	1	1
2	2	2	2	2	2
3	3	3	3	3	3
4	4	4	4	4	4
5	5	5	5	5	5
6	6	6	6	6	6
7	7	7	7	7	7
8	8	8	8	8	8
9	9	9	9	9	9
10	10	10	10	10	10
11	11	11	11	11	11
12	12	12	12	12	12
13	13	13	13	13	13
14	14	14	14	14	14
15	15	15	15	15	15
16	16	16	16	16	16
17	17	17	17	17	17
18	18	18	18	18	18
19	19	19	19	19	19
20	20	20	20	20	20
21	21	21	21	21	21
22	22	22	22	22	22
23	23	23	23	23	23
24	24	24	24	24	24
25	25	25	25	25	25
26	26	26	26	26	26
27	27	27	27	27	27
28	28	28	28	28	28
29	29	29	29	29	29
30		30	30	30	30
31		31		31	

Date Begun _____

July	Aug.	Sept.	Oct.	Nov.	Dec.
1	1	1	1	1	1
2	2	2	2	2	2
3	3	3	3	3	3
4	4	4	4	4	4
5	5	5	5	5	5
6	6	6	6	6	6
7	7	7	7	7	7
8	8	8	8	8	8
9	9	9	9	9	9
10	10	10	10	10	10
11	11	11	11	11	11
12	12	12	12	12	12
13	13	13	13	13	13
14	14	14	14	14	14
15	15	15	15	15	15
16	16	16	16	16	16
17	17	17	17	17	17
18	18	18	18	18	18
19	19	19	19	19	19
20	20	20	20	20	20
21	21	21	21	21	21
22	22	22	22	22	22
23	23	23	23	23	23
24	24	24	24	24	24
25	25	25	25	25	25
26	26	26	26	26	26
27	27	27	27	27	27
28	28	28	28	28	28
29	29	29	29	29	29
30	30	30	30	30	30
31	31		31		31

Notes

Dedication

1. Roy B. Zuck, *The Speaker's Quote Book*, citing J. Wilbur Chapman (Grand Rapids, MI: Kregel, 1997), p. 39.

Chapter 2—First Things First

1. John MacArthur, Jr., *The MacArthur New Testament Commentary* (Chicago: Moody Press, 1995), p. 162.

2. This quote is frequently attributed to D.L. Moody; however, the origin of it is unconfirmed.

3. *God's Words of Life for Teens*, NIV (Grand Rapids, MI: Inspirio, 2000), p. 29.

Chapter 3—Stories for Your Heart

1. *Life Application Bible—*TLB (Wheaton, IL: Tyndale House, 1988), p. 9.

2. *Life Application Bible*, p. 9.

Chapter 4—True Beauty

1. *Ryrie Study Bible* (Chicago, IL: Moody Press, 1977), p. 736.

2. *Life Application Bible*, p. 776.

3. Kendrick, Michael and Daryl Lucas, eds., *365 Life Lessons from Bible People—A Life Application Devotional* (Wheaton, IL: Tyndale House, 1996), p. 209.

4. William Hersey Davis, "Reputation and Character," source unknown.

Chapter 5—Finding a Role Model, Part 1

1. *Life Application Bible*, NLT (Wheaton, IL: Tyndale, 2000).

2. *God's Words of Life for Teens*, NIV (Grand Rapids, MI: Zondervan, 2000), p. 45.

Chapter 6—Finding a Role Model, Part 2

1. James Strong, *Exhaustive Concordance of the Bible* (Nashville, TN: Abingdon Press, 1973), p. 39.

Chapter 7—Finding a Role Model, Part 3

1. Elizabeth George, *Beautiful in God's Eyes for Young Women* (Eugene, OR: Harvest House, 2014), p. 150.

2. Ray and Anne Ortlund, *The Best Half of Life* (Glendale, CA: Regal Books, 1976), p. 88.

3. Roy B. Zuck, *The Speaker's Quote Book* (Grand Rapids, MI: Kregel, 1997), p. 174.

4. Robert L. Alden, *Proverbs—A Commentary on an Ancient Book of Timeless Advice* (Grand Rapids, MI: Baker Book House, 1990), p. 222.

5. George, *Beautiful in God's Eyes for Young Women*, p. 175.

Chapter 8—Following After God's Own Heart

1. Elizabeth George, *A Young Woman After God's Own Heart* (Eugene, OR: Harvest House Publishers, 2003).

2. *Life Application Bible—The Living Bible* (Wheaton, IL: Tyndale House, 1988), p. 1466.

Chapter 9—Walking by the Spirit

1. Elizabeth George, *A Young Woman's Walk with God* (Eugene, OR: Harvest House, 2006), p. 29.

2. George, *A Young Woman's Walk with God,* p. 41.

3. George, *A Young Woman's Walk with God,* p. 52.

4. George, *A Young Woman's Walk with God,* p. 80.

5. Elizabeth George, *A Woman's Walk with God* (Eugene, OR: Harvest House, 2000), p. 94.

6. George, *A Woman's Walk with God,* p. 105.

7. John Wesley, as cited in George, *A Young Woman's Walk with God,* pp. 107-8.

8. Donald K. Campbell, as cited in George, *A Woman's Walk with God,* p. 148.

9. D.L. Moody, *Notes from My Bible and Thoughts from My Library,* quoting Bowen (Grand Rapids, MI: Baker Book House, 1979), p. 114.

10. Dan Baumann, *Extraordinary Living for Ordinary People* (Irvine, CA: Harvest House, 1978), pp. 118-19, as cited in George, *A Young Woman's Walk with God,* p. 163.

Chapter 10—Becoming More Like Jesus

1. Elizabeth George, *A Young Woman Who Reflects the Heart of Jesus* (Eugene, OR: Harvest House, 2011).

A Young Woman After God's Own Heart

Elizabeth George

Over 350,000 Sold

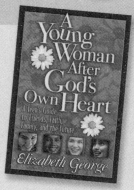

What does it mean to live God in your everyday life? It means knowing and following God's perfect plan for you as a young woman. Learn how to...

- grow close to God
- get along with family and friends
- make the right kinds of choices
- become more like Jesus
- prepare for the future

In this book you'll find yourself caught up in the exciting adventure of a lifetime—that of becoming a young woman after God's own heart!

Get the Devotional Too!

Did you know God has lots to say about your dreams, hopes, worries, and fears? In these devotions you'll discover how to trust God and live out your faith, and grow daily in beauty and confidence. Don't miss this incredible, life-changing journey to God's heart.

More Books That Speak to the Hearts of Young Christian Women

HARVEST HOUSE PUBLISHERS
EUGENE, OREGON

BIBLE STUDIES *for* BUSY WOMEN

Character Studies

Old Testament Studies

New Testament Studies

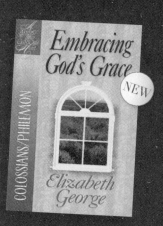

Books by Elizabeth George

- Beautiful in God's Eyes
- Beautiful in God's Eyes for Young Women
- Breaking the Worry Habit…Forever
- Finding God's Path Through Your Trials
- Following God with All Your Heart
- The Heart of a Woman Who Prays
- Life Management for Busy Women
- Loving God with All Your Mind
- Loving God with All Your Mind DVD and Workbook
- A Mom After God's Own Heart
- A Mom After God's Own Heart Devotional
- Moments of Grace for a Woman's Heart
- One-Minute Inspiration for Women
- Prayers to Calm Your Heart
- Quiet Confidence for a Woman's Heart
- Raising a Daughter After God's Own Heart
- The Remarkable Women of the Bible
- Small Changes for a Better Life
- Walking with the Women of the Bible
- A Wife After God's Own Heart
- A Woman After God's Own Heart®
- A Woman After God's Own Heart®— Daily Devotional
- A Woman After God's Own Heart® Deluxe Edition
- A Woman's Daily Walk with God
- A Woman's Guide to Making Right Choices
- A Woman's High Calling
- A Woman's Walk with God
- A Woman Who Reflects the Heart of Jesus
- A Young Woman After God's Own Heart
- A Young Woman After God's Own Heart— A Devotional
- A Young Woman's Guide to Discovering Her Bible
- A Young Woman's Guide to Making Right Choices
- A Young Woman's Guide to Prayer
- A Young Woman Who Reflects the Heart of Jesus

Study Guides

- Beautiful in God's Eyes Growth & Study Guide
- Finding God's Path Through Your Trials Growth & Study Guide
- Following God with All Your Heart Growth & Study Guide
- Life Management for Busy Women Growth & Study Guide
- Loving God with All Your Mind Growth & Study Guide
- Loving God with All Your Mind Interactive Workbook
- A Mom After God's Own Heart Growth & Study Guide
- The Remarkable Women of the Bible Growth & Study Guide
- Small Changes for a Better Life Growth & Study Guide
- A Wife After God's Own Heart Growth & Study Guide
- A Woman After God's Own Heart® Growth & Study Guide
- A Woman's Call to Prayer Growth & Study Guide
- A Woman's High Calling Growth & Study Guide
- A Woman Who Reflects the Heart of Jesus Growth & Study Guide

Children's Books

- A Girl After God's Own Heart
- A Girl After God's Own Heart Devotional
- A Girl's Guide to Making Really Good Choices
- God's Wisdom for Little Girls
- A Little Girl After God's Own Heart

Books by Jim George

- 10 Minutes to Knowing the Men and Women of the Bible
- The Bare Bones Bible® Handbook
- The Bare Bones Bible® Handbook for Teens
- A Boy After God's Own Heart
- A Boy's Guide to Making Really Good Choices
- A Dad After God's Own Heart
- A Husband After God's Own Heart
- Know Your Bible from A to Z
- A Leader After God's Own Heart
- A Man After God's Own Heart
- A Man After God's Own Heart Devotional
- The Man Who Makes a Difference
- One-Minute Insights for Men
- A Young Man After God's Own Heart
- A Young Man's Guide to Discovering His Bible
- A Young Man's Guide to Making Right Choices

Books by Jim & Elizabeth George

- A Couple After God's Own Heart
- A Couple After God's Own Heart Interactive Workbook
- God's Wisdom for Little Boys
- A Little Boy After God's Own Heart

About the Author

Elizabeth George is a bestselling author who has more than 8 million books in print and is a popular speaker at Christian women's events. Her passion is to teach the Bible in a way that changes women's lives.

For information about Elizabeth's ministry or to purchase her books, visit her website:

www.ElizabethGeorge.com